Lincoln's joke honesty, his deprecation a̲ ̲ ̲ ̲ ̲. This collection brings a fascinating Lincoln to life. You'll find accounts about his grief over the death of his beloved Anne Rutledge, his startling premonition about his assassination, and the challenges of the Civil War, which pushed Lincoln to blistering satire as well as to sorrow. Browsing through this unique volume you'll encounter a man and his times in all their complexity, including selections like:

GOVERNMENT: "No man is good enough to govern another man without the other's consent."

FUTURE: "The best thing about the future is that it only comes one day at a time."

THE WIT AND WISDOM
OF ABRAHAM LINCOLN

ALEX AYRES is the editor of *The Wit and Wisdom of Mark Twain* (also available in a Meridian edition) and a former editor of *Running Times* and *The Harvard Lampoon*. His epigrams have appeared in *Forbes*.

The Wit and Wisdom

—of—

ABRAHAM LINCOLN

EDITED BY

ALEX AYRES

A MERIDIAN BOOK

MERIDIAN
Published by the Penguin Group
Penguin Group (USA) Inc., 375 Hudson Street, New York, New York 10014, U.S.A.
• Penguin Group (Canada), 90 Eglinton Avenue East, Suite 700, Toronto,
Ontario, Canada M4P 2Y3 (a division of Pearson Penguin Canada Inc.) • Penguin
Books Ltd., 80 Strand, London WC2R 0RL, England • Penguin Ireland, 25 St.
Stephen's Green, Dublin 2, Ireland (a division of Penguin Books Ltd.) • Penguin
Group (Australia), 250 Camberwell Road, Camberwell, Victoria 3124, Australia
(a division of Pearson Australia Group Pty. Ltd.) • Penguin Books India Pvt.
Ltd., 11 Community Centre, Panchsheel Park, New Delhi – 110 017, India •
Penguin Group (NZ), 67 Apollo Drive, Rosedale, North Shore 0632, New Zealand
(a division of Pearson New Zealand Ltd.) • Penguin Books (South Africa) (Pty.)
Ltd., 24 Sturdee Avenue, Rosebank, Johannesburg 2196, South Africa

Penguin Books Ltd., Registered Offices: 80 Strand, London WC2R 0RL, England.

First published by Meridian, a member of Penguin Group (USA) Inc.

First Printing, February 1992
25 24 23 22 21 20

ⓜ REGISTERED TRADEMARK—MARCA REGISTRADA

LIBRARY OF CONGRESS CATALOGING-IN-PUBLICATION DATA

Lincoln, Abraham, 1809–1865.
   The wit and wisdom of Abraham Lincoln / edited by Alex Ayres.
      p.   cm.
   ISBN 978-0-452-01089-5
   1. Lincoln, Abraham, 1809–1865—Quotations.   2. Lincoln, Abraham, 1809–1865—Humor.   I. Title.
E457.99.L55   1992
973.7'092—dc20   91–25678

Printed in the United States of America

To the towering spirit

ACKNOWLEDGMENTS

Thanks to Abraham Lincoln—arguably our greatest president but unquestionably our *funniest* president—for the inspiration. Thanks to Pam Ayres, Hy Cohen, Arnold Dolin, Hugh Rawson, Julia Moskin, the Lincoln scholars who have kept it alive, the Lincoln lovers who have passed it on, and thanks to you—the reader—for taking it in your hand, if only for a moment.

EXPLANATORY NOTE

Abraham Lincoln is remembered as a tragic figure, a martyred emancipator. But he is also a great comic figure. Comedy was married to tragedy in his life and his personality.

It was the wit and wisdom of Abraham Lincoln that first won him the hearts of the people. Prior to his election as president in 1860 he never held a higher post than that of a one-term Illinois congressman. But people trusted Lincoln instinctively because he seemed wiser than other men, and they liked him because he was *funnier* than other men.

Abraham Lincoln was a great writer and a great orator as well as a great leader. He deserves a place in American literature as well as history. However, he wrote no books, he composed no memoirs, he left behind no magnum opus. The quotations cited in this book are drawn from a variety of sources, both oral and written.

The Wit and Wisdom of Abraham Lincoln includes both stories told about Lincoln and stories told by Lincoln.

No president has had more stories told about him than Lincoln. Many of these stories have passed from American history into American folklore. Sometimes it is hard to separate Lincoln the historical figure from Lincoln the folk hero. He is shown here in both roles.

No president told more stories than Lincoln. He was the storytelling president. He used anecdotes the way Christ is said to have used parables, to make a point, to illustrate a principle. He used humor the way Mark Twain used humor, to break down barriers and throw light on the truth.

Ultimately it's for you to decide if the stories told about Lincoln are true and if the stories told by Lincoln contain truth.

The Wit and Wisdom of Abraham Lincoln is for anyone who would like to know what Lincoln said to us—and what he is saying to us today.

ON ABRAHAM LINCOLN

There lies the most perfect ruler of men who ever lived.

—Edwin M. Stanton
Lincoln's Secretary of War

Lincoln, with all his foibles, is the greatest character since Christ.

—John Hay
Lincoln's private secretary

Lincoln is the best loved man that ever trod this continent.

—Theodore Cuyler
Clergyman and author

If one would know the greatness of Lincoln one should listen to the stories which are told about him in other parts of the world. I have been in wild places where one hears the name of America uttered with such mystery as if it were some heaven or hell . . . but I heard this only in connection with the name Lincoln.

—Leo Tolstoy

But you have not told us a syllable about the greatest general and greatest ruler of the world. We want to know something about him. He was a hero. He spoke with a voice of thunder, he laughed like the sunrise and his deeds were strong as the rock and as sweet as the fragrance of roses. . . . He was so great that he even forgave the crimes of his greatest enemies and shook brotherly hands with those who had plotted against his life. His name was Lincoln and the country in which he lived is called America. . . . Tell us of that man.

—Tribal chief in Russia's Caucasus to Leo Tolstoy

Mr. Lincoln's wit and mirth will give him a passport to the thoughts and hearts of millions who would take no interest in the sterner and more practical parts of his character.

—George S. Boutwell
Secretary of U.S. Treasury under Grant

Mr. Lincoln's flow of humor was a sparkling spring, gushing out of a rock—the flashing water had a somber background which made it all the brighter.

—Petroleum Nasby
Lincoln's favorite humorist

Many of Mr. Lincoln's stories were as apt and instructive as the best of Aesop's Fables.

—Hugh McCullough
Lincoln's Secretary of Treasury

Mr. Lincoln's resources as a story-teller were inexhaustible, and no condition could arise in a case beyond his capacity to furnish an illustration with an appropriate anecdote.

—Lawrence Weldon
U.S. Court of Claims Judge
during Lincoln administration

Mr. Lincoln was recognized as the champion story-teller of the Capitol.

—Benjamin Poore
Editor of The Congressional Record

He raised the wisecrack to the level of scripture.

—B. A. Botkin
American folklore scholar

Now his simple and weighty words will be gathered like those of Washington, and your children, and your children's children, shall be taught to ponder the simplicity and deep wisdom of utterances which, in their time, passed, in party heat, as idle words.

—Reverend Henry Ward Beecher
Clergyman and author

Strange mingling of mirth and tears, of the tragic and grotesque, of cap and crown, of Socrates and Rabelais, of Aesop and Marcus Aurelius—Lincoln, the gentlest memory of the world.

—Robert G. Ingersoll
Lawyer, orator, author

Abraham Lincoln . . . was at home and welcome with the humblest, and had a spirit and a practical vein in the times of terror that commanded the admiration of the wisest. His heart was as great as the world, but there was no room in it to hold the memory of a wrong.

—Ralph Waldo Emerson

This dust was once the man,
Gentle, plain, just and resolute, under whose cautious hand
Against the foulest crime in history known in any land or age,
Was saved the Union of these States.

—Walt Whitman

Lincoln was a very normal man with very normal gifts, but all upon a great scale, all knit together in loose and natural form, like the great frame in which he moved and dwelt.

—Woodrow Wilson

Lincoln's words have become the common covenant of our public life. Let us now get on with his work.

—Lyndon Johnson

If it wasn't for Abe, I'd still be on the open market.

—Dick Gregory
Black activist and comedian

THE WIT AND WISDOM
OF ABRAHAM LINCOLN

ADVICE

Better to remain silent and be thought a fool than to speak out and remove all doubt.

—Attributed to both Abraham Lincoln and Mark Twain

My advice . . . is to keep cool.

—Speech, Pittsburgh, February 14, 1861

Beware of rashness, but with energy and sleepless vigilance go forward and give us victories.

—Letter to Major General Joseph Hooker,
January 26, 1863

Now, as to the young men. You must not wait to be brought forward by the older men. For instance, do you suppose that I should have ever got into notice if I had waited to be hunted up and pushed forward by older men?

—Letter to William H. Herndon, June 22, 1848
(see COUNSELORS, LAWYERS)

3

AGRICULTURE

"No other human occupation opens so wide a field for the profitable and agreeable combination of labor with cultivated thought, as agriculture," Abraham Lincoln declared in a speech before the Wisconsin Agricultural Society on September 30, 1859. "Every blade of grass is a study; and to produce two, where there was but one, is both a profit and a pleasure."

Lincoln then told a little parable. "An Eastern monarch once charged his wise men to invent him a sentence to be ever in view, and which should be true and appropriate in all times and situations. They presented him the words: *And this, too, shall pass away.* How much it expresses! How chastening in the hour of pride! How consoling in the depths of affliction!

"And yet let us hope it is not *quite* true. Let us hope, rather, that by the best cultivation of the physical world beneath and around us, and the intellectual and moral world within us, we shall secure an individual, social and political prosperity and happiness, whose course shall be onward and upward, and which, while the earth endures, shall not pass away."

AID

In a desperate predicament, it is human nature to turn to any available source of aid, however unreliable.

President Lincoln was reading over a stack of telegrams from General George B. McClellan pleading for more troops and more supplies. "It appears to me that poor McClellan has got himself lost," remarked Lincoln. "He's been hollering for help ever since he began his Southern campaign. I think he wants somebody to come to his deliverance and rescue him from the place he's got into.

"He reminds me of the story of a man out in Illinois who visited the state penitentiary in company with a few friends. They took a tour of the institution and saw all the facilities, but near the end of the tour this fellow got separated from his friends and couldn't find his way out.

"He roamed up and down one cold prison corridor after another, becoming more desperate with each passing minute, when, at last, he came across a convict who was peering out from between the bars of his cell door. Here was salvation at last. Breathing a sigh of relief, the man hurried up to the prisoner and hastily inquired, " 'Say, pal! How do you get out of this place?' "

(see ASSISTANCE, GENERALS, MCCLELLAN)

ALCOHOLISM

The demon of intemperance ever seems to have delighted in sucking the blood of genius and of generosity.

—Temperance Address, February 22, 1842
to the Springfield Washington Temperance Society,
Springfield, Illinois

ALGER, HORATIO

Horatio Alger was a nineteenth-century novelist whose name has become synonymous with the moral version of the American dream: the rags-to-riches tale of the good-hearted poor boy who makes good.

The heroes of Horatio Alger's dime novels were always underprivileged youths who won fame and wealth through practicing civic virtues, such as honesty, diligence, and perseverance. Alger's many novels sold mil-

5

lions of copies and influenced American youths by stressing merit, rather than birth or background, as the secret of success.

Abraham Lincoln, of course, was the real-life model for the Horatio Alger hero. His "log cabin to White House" success story epitomizes the Horatio Alger sequence, which is similar to the fairy-tale pattern. Abe Lincoln is the proof of the Alger maxim that "any boy can become president."

Horatio Alger wrote a biography of Lincoln, *Abraham Lincoln, The Backwoods Boy; or How a Young Rail-Splitter Became President* (1883), which shows how Lincoln's life has provided a text from which American pulpiteers can preach. This excerpt illustrates Lincoln's proverbial honesty:

> A woman entered the store and asked for half a pound of tea. The young clerk weighed it out, and handed it to her in a parcel. This was the last sale of the day.
>
> The next morning, when commencing his duties, Abe discovered a four-ounce weight on the scales. It flashed upon him at once that he had used this in the sale of the night previous, and so, of course, given his customer short weight. I am afraid there are many country merchants who would not have been much worried by this discovery. Not so the young clerk in whom we are interested. He weighed out the balance of the half pound, shut up store, and carried it to the defrauded customer. I think my young readers will begin to see that the name so often given, in later times, to President Lincoln, of "Honest Old Abe," was well deserved. A man who begins by strict honesty in his youth is not likely to change as he grows older, and mercantile honesty is some guarantee of political honesty.

Young Abe Lincoln was a storekeeper for a year in New Salem, Illinois. A fact not mentioned in the Horatio Alger history is that the store went out of business and

Lincoln was left with a debt he was not able to pay off in full until 1848, nearly two decades later.

(see HONEST ABE)

ALIENS

In 1854, when Abraham Lincoln was campaigning on his unsuccessful bid for the Illinois Senate seat, he received the endorsement of the Know-Nothings, who thought only native-born Americans should have rights. Declining their endorsement, Lincoln said in defense of aliens:

"Who are the native Americans? Do they not wear the breechcloth and carry the tomahawk? We pushed them from their homes, and now turn upon others not fortunate enough to come over as early as our forefathers. Gentlemen, your party is wrong in principle."

Then he told this story: "I had an Irishman named Patrick cultivating my garden. One morning I went out to see how he was getting along. 'Mr. Lincoln, what do yez think of these Know-Nothings?' he asked. I explained what they were trying to do, and asked Pat why he had not been born in America. 'Faith,' he replied, 'I wanted to but my mother would not let me.' "

AMBIGUITY

A successful politician must be a master of ambiguity. President Lincoln was quite accustomed to ambiguity; it did not disconcert him.

On one occasion the president and some members of his cabinet were with the army south of Washington when they were joined by Secretary of War Edwin M. Stanton. Stanton said that just before he left Washington he received a telegram from General Ormsby M.

Mitchel in Alabama, asking instructions to cope with a military emergency.

"I am afraid that I did not precisely understand the nature of the emergency explained by General Mitchel, but I answered back, 'All right, go ahead,' " Secretary Stanton told President Lincoln. "Now, Mr. President, if I have made an error in not understanding him correctly, I will have to get you to countermand the order."

Presented with this puzzle, President Lincoln cleared his throat. "Well," he said, "that is very similar to the circumstances of a certain horse sale that I remember took place at the crossroads down in Kentucky, when I was a boy.

"A particularly fine horse was to be sold, and a large crowd had assembled to witness the spectacle. They had a small boy to ride the horse up and down while the spectators examined the horse's points.

"As the boy paraded past, one old man called out: 'Look here, boy, hain't that horse got the splints?'

"The boy replied: 'Mister, I don't know what the splints is, but if it's good for him, he has got it; if it ain't good for him, he ain't got it.'

"Now," concluded the president, "if this was good for Mitchel, it was all right; but if it was not, I shall have countermanded it."

AMBITION

Every man is said to have his peculiar ambition . . . I have no other so great as that of being truly esteemed of my fellow-men, by rendering myself worthy of their esteem.

—Communication to the people of Sangamo County
(Illinois), March 9, 1832

You know better than any man living that from my boy-hood up my ambition was to be President.

—Lamon, *Recollections of Abraham Lincoln, 1847–1865*
[Ward Lamon was Lincoln's law partner
in the 1850s.]
(see PRESIDENCY)

AMERICA, UNITED STATES OF

"Most governments have been based, practically, on the denial of equal rights of men," wrote Abraham Lincoln in an essay on slavery on July 1, 1854. "Ours began by affirming those rights. They said, some men are too ignorant and vicious to share in government. Possibly so, said we; and, by your system, you would always keep them ignorant and vicious. We proposed to give all a chance; and we expected the weak to grow stronger, the ignorant wiser and all better and happier together. We made the experiment, and the fruit is before us."

Lincoln never tried to redefine America; rather, he tried to reaffirm the original definition given to the nation by the Founding Fathers. "They knew the tendency of prosperity to breed tyrants, and so they established these great self-evident truths, that when in the distant future some man, some faction, some interest, should set up the doctrine that none but rich men, or none but white men, were entitled to life, liberty, and the pursuit of happiness, their posterity might look up again to the Declaration of Independence and take courage to renew the battle which their fathers began."

No president since the time of Washington and Jefferson has been closer in spirit to the Founding Fathers than has Lincoln. His political principles were not new; they were essentially the principles of Jefferson and Washington, adapted to his own time. It was with deep-

9

felt reverence that he invoked their memory at the beginning of his greatest speech: "Four score and seven years ago our fathers set forth on this continent a new nation, conceived in liberty and dedicated to the proposition that all men are created equal."

What Lincoln accomplished was not only the preservation of that Union first formed by the Founders from the most serious threat in the history of the nation but' the reestablishment of the nation itself on its founding principles—in practice as well as in theory. The Emancipation Proclamation removed the greatest barrier to a true and faithful observance of the Declaration of Independence and its charter principles of equality and liberty for all. Lincoln continued the work started by the Founders, preserving what they established and realizing one of their greatest unfulfilled dreams. For this achievement Lincoln should be recognized not only as a great successor to the Founders of America, but as *one of them*.

I hold that, in contemplation of universal law and of the Constitution, the Union of these States is perpetual.

—First Inaugural Address, March 4, 1861

As a nation of freemen we must live through all time, or die by suicide.

—Speech, Springfield, Illinois, January 27, 1838

What constitutes the bulwark of our own liberty and independence? It is not our frowning battlements, our bristling sea coasts. . . . Our reliance is in the love of liberty which God has planted in us. Our defense is in the spirit which prized liberty as the heritage of all men, in all lands everywhere.

—Speech, Edwardsville, Illinois, September 13, 1858

Many free countries have lost their liberty, and ours may lose hers: but if she shall, be it my proudest plume, not that I was the last to desert, but that I never deserted her.

—Speech, Springfield, Illinois, December, 1839

At what point then is the approach of danger to be expected? I answer if it ever reach us it must spring up amongst us; it cannot come from abroad. If destruction be our lot, we must ourselves be its author and finisher.

—Speech, Springfield, Illinois, January 27, 1838

We here highly resolve that these dead shall not have died in vain, that this nation shall have a new birth of freedom.

—Gettysburg Address, November 19, 1863

We shall prove, in a very few years, that we are indeed the treasury of the world.

—Letter to coal miners, conveyed by Schuyler Colfax (written hours before Lincoln's death, April 14, 1865) (see CIVIL WAR, DECLARATION OF INDEPENDENCE, DEMOCRACY, EQUALITY, LIBERTY)

AMERICANS

We are not enemies, but friends. We must not be enemies. Though passion may have strained, it must not break our bonds of affection. The mystic chords of memory, stretching from every battlefield and patriot grave to every living heart and hearthstone all over this broad land, will yet swell the chorus of the Union when again touched, as surely they will be, by the better angels of our nature.

—First Inaugural Address, March 4, 1861 (see ENEMIES, FRIENDS)

ANARCHY

Plainly, the central idea of secession is the essence of anarchy. A majority held in restraint by constitutional checks and limitations, and always changing easily with deliberate changes of popular opinions and sentiments, is the only true sovereign of a free people. Whoever rejects it does, of necessity, fly to anarchy.

—First Inaugural Address, March 4, 1861
(see SECESSION)

ANCESTRY

Abraham Lincoln's innate sense of democracy was so strong that he habitually brushed off questions about his ancestry, even though his Quaker ancestors included colonial governors and others of distinction.

"I don't know who my grandfather was," he said. "I am much more concerned to know what his grandson will be."

(see TITLES)

ANGER

Secretary of War Edwin M. Stanton had a terrible temper. One day President Lincoln found Stanton fuming over a letter the latter had received from a major general accusing him of favoritism. The president advised Stanton to sit down and pour all his anger into a letter. "Prick him hard! Score him deeply, Stanton," said Lincoln. "It will do you good."

Stanton sat down and wrote the most abusive, vitriolic letter that a fierce and furious mind could conceive. When the letter was finished, President Lincoln asked Stanton to read it to him. "First rate!" exclaimed Lincoln, praising its pique.

Pleased at this commendation, Stanton began folding the letter to fit in an envelope.

"What are you going to do with it now?" asked Lincoln.

"Why, I'm going to dispatch it, of course," said Stanton.

Lincoln shook his head. "Nonsense! You don't want to send that letter. *Put it in the stove!* That's the way I do when I have written a letter while I am mad. It 's a good letter, Stanton, and you've had a good time writing it, and feel better. Now, burn it, and write again."

(see QUARRELING)

If the great American people will only keep their temper on both sides of the line, the troubles will come to an end.

—Speech, Pittsburgh, February 14, 1861

APPLICANTS

As soon as he took up residence at the White House, President Lincoln was swamped with requests for government appointments. "This human struggle and scramble for office, for a way to live without work, will finally test the strength of our institutions," he warned.

The volume of applications from office seekers was so staggering that it became an onerous burden to Lincoln.

"What is the matter, Mr. Lincoln?" inquired a friend one day, who saw the president looking sad and dispirited. "Has anything gone wrong at the front?"

"No," replied Lincoln, with a weary smile. "It isn't the war. It's the post office at Brownsville, Missouri."

Responding to the swarms of job applicants was a wearying task that severely tested Lincoln's powers of diplomacy, as well as his sense of humor.

To an applicant for a post that had already been filled, Lincoln sent this telegraph: "What nation do you desire General Allen to be made quarter-master-general of? This nation already has a quarter-master-general.— A. Lincoln."

There were not nearly enough jobs for all the qualified applicants, to say nothing of the more numerous unqualified applicants. One afternoon at a White House reception, President Lincoln was accosted by a group of applicants. He fended them off with a genial rejoinder that made the men grin and the ladies blush:

"Now, gentlemen, I will tell you the truth. I have thousands of applications like this, and it is impossible to satisfy all. These positions are like office-seekers— there are too many pigs for the teats."

(see HAWAII, JACKASS, OFFICE-SEEKERS)

ARGUMENT

A specious and fantastic arrangement of words, by which a man can prove a horse-chestnut to be a chestnut horse.

—Speech, Ottawa, Illinois, August 21, 1858
(see CRISIS, EXPLANATIONS)

ART

President Lincoln was once shown a painting that was perhaps ahead of its time in its nonrepresentational departure from the laws of perspective and proportion.

Asked his opinion of the canvas, Lincoln cleared his throat. "Why, the painter is a very good painter. He observes the Lord's commandments."

"What do you mean by that, sir?"

"It seems to me," Lincoln answered thoughtfully, "that he hath not made to himself the likeness of any-

thing that is in the heaven above, or that is in the earth
beneath or that is in the waters under the earth.''

(see PORTRAIT)

ASSASSINATION

Perhaps the best single account of the assassination of
President Lincoln on April 14, 1865, was written by Walt
Whitman, the greatest American poet of the age, in *Portraits of Lincoln:*

The day seems to have been a pleasant one throughout
the whole land—the moral atmosphere pleasant, too—the
long storm, so dark, so fratricidal, full of blood and doubt
and gloom, over and ended at last by the sunrise of such
an absolute national victory, and utter breaking down of
secessionism—we almost doubted our senses! Lee had ca-
pitulated, beneath the apple tree at Appomattox. The
other armies, the flanges of the revolt, swiftly followed.

And could it really be, then? Out of all the affairs of
this world of woe and passion, of failure and disorder
and dismay, was there really come the confirmed, unerr-
ing sign of peace, like a shaft of pure light—of rightful
rule—of God?

But I must not dwell on accessories. The deed hastens.
The popular afternoon paper, the little Evening Star, had
scattered all over its third page, divided among the ad-
vertisements in a sensational manner in a hundred different paces: 'The President and his lady will be at the
theatre this evening.'

Lincoln was fond of the theatre. I have myself seen him
there several times. I remember thinking how funny it
was that he, the leading actor in the greatest and storm-
iest drama known to real history's stage, through centu-
ries, should sit there and be so completely interested in
those human jackstraws, moving about with their silly
little gestures, foreign spirit, and flatulent text.

So the day, as I say, was propitious. Early herbage,
early flowers, were out. I remember where I was stop-

ping at the time, the season being advanced, there were many lilacs in full bloom. By one of those caprices that enter and give tinge to events without being a part of them, I find myself always reminded of the great tragedy of this day by the sight and odor of these blossoms. It never fails.

On this occasion the theatre was crowded, many ladies in rich and gay costumes, officers in their uniforms, many well-known citizens, young folks, the usual cluster of gas lights, the usual magnetism of so many people, cheerful with perfumes, music of violins and flutes—and overall, that saturating, that vast, vague wonder, Victory, the nation's victory, the triumph of the Union, filling the air, the thought, the sense, with exhilaration more than all the perfumes.

The President came betimes, and, with his wife, witnessed the play from the large stage boxes of the second tier, two thrown into one, and profusely draped with the national flag. The acts and scenes of the piece—one of those singularly witless compositions which have at the least the merit of giving entire relief to an audience engaged in mental action or business excitements during the day, as it makes not the slightest call on either the moral, emotional, esthetic or spiritual nature—a piece in which among other characters, so called, a Yankee—certainly such a one as was never seen, or at least like it ever seen in North America, is introduced in England, with a varied fol-de-rol of talk, plot, scenery, and such phantasmagoria as goes to make up a modern popular drama—had progressed perhaps through a couple of its acts, when, in the midst of this comedy, or tragedy, or non-such, or whatever it is to be called, and to offset it, or finish it out, as if in Nature's and the Great Muses's mockery of these poor mimics, comes interpolated that scene, not really or exactly to be described at all (for on the many hundreds who were there it seems at this hour to have left little but a passing blur, a dream, a blotch)—and yet partially described as I now proceed to give it:

There is a scene in the play, representing the modern parlor, in which two unprecedented ladies are informed by the unprecedented and impossible Yankee that he is not a man of fortune, and therefore undesirable for marriage-catching purposes; after which, the comments being finished, the dramatic trio make exit, leaving the stage clear for a moment.

There was a pause, a hush as it were. At this period came the death of Abraham Lincoln.

Great as that was, with all its manifold train circling around it, and stretching into the future for many a century, in the politics, history, art, etc. of the New World, in point of fact, the main thing, the actual murder, transpired with the quiet and simplicity of the commonest occurrence—the bursting of a bud or pod in the growth of vegetation, for instance.

Through the general hum following the stage pause, with the change of positions, etc., came the muffled sound of a pistol shot, which not one hundredth part of the audience heard at the time—and yet a moment's hush—somehow, surely a vague, startled thrill—and then, through the ornamented, draperied, starred and striped space-way of the President's box, a sudden figure, a man, raises himself with hands and feet, stands a moment on the railing, leaps below to the stage, falls out of position, catching his boot-heel in the copious drapery (the American flag), falls on one knee, quickly recovers himself, rises as if nothing had happened (he really sprains his ankle, unfelt then)—and the figure, Booth, the murderer, dressed in plain black broadcloth, bareheaded, with a full head of glossy, raven hair, and his eyes, like some mad animal's, flashing with light and resolution, yet with a certain strange calmness holds aloft in one hand a large knife—walks along not much back of the footlights—turns fully towards the audience, his face of statuesque beauty, lit by those basilisk eyes, flashing with desperation, perhaps insanity—launches out in a firm and steady voice the words, 'Sic semper tyrannis'—and then walks with neither slow nor very rapid pace diagonally across to the back of the stage, and disappears. (Had not all this terrible scene—making the mimic ones preposterous—had it not all been rehearsed, in blank, by Booth, beforehand?)

17

A moment's hush, incredulous—a scream—a cry of murder—Mrs. Lincoln leaning out of the box, with ashy cheeks and lips, with involuntary cry, pointing to the retreating figure, "He has killed the President!"

And still a moment's strange, incredulous suspense—and then the deluge!—then that mixture of horror, noises, uncertainty—the sound, somewhere back, of a horse's hoofs clattering with speed—the people burst through chairs and railings, and break them up—that noise adds to the queerness of the scene—there is inextricable confusion and terror—women faint—quite feeble persons fall, and are trampled on—many cries of agony are heard—the broad stage suddenly fills to suffocation with a dense and motley crowd, like some horrible carnival—the audience rush generally upon it—at least the strong men do—the actors and actresses are there in their play costumes and painted faces, with mortal fright showing through the rouge—some trembling, some in tears—the screams and calls, confused talk—redoubled, trebled—two or three manage to pass up water from the stage to the President's box, others try to clamber up, etc., etc.

In the midst of all this the soldiers of the President's Guard, with others, suddenly drawn to the scene, burst in—some two hundred altogether—they storm the house, through all the tiers, especially the upper ones—inflamed with fury, literally charging the audience with fixed bayonets, muskets and pistols, shouting, "Clear out! Clear out!" . . .

Outside, too, in the atmosphere of shock and craze, crowds of people filled with frenzy, ready to seize any outlet for it, came near committing murder several times on innocent individuals. . . .

And in the midst of that night pandemonium of senseless hate, infuriated soldiers, the audience and the crowd—the stage, and all its actors and actresses, its paint pots, spangles, gas-light—the life-blood from those veins, the best and sweetest of the land, drips slowly down, and death's ooze already begins its little bubbles on the lips.

Such, hurriedly sketched, were the accompaniments of

the death of President Lincoln. So suddenly, and in murder and horror unsurpassed, he was taken from us.

(see also BOOTH, DEATH,
KENNEDY ASSASSINATION PARALLELS)

ASSISTANCE

President Lincoln preferred generals who were self-sufficient and did not perpetually appeal to Washington for more assistance.

General Ulysses S. Grant offered this recollection of the day he received his appointment from President Lincoln:

Just after receiving my commission as lieutenant-general the president called me aside to speak to me privately. After a brief reference to the military situation, he said he thought he could illustrate what he wanted to say by a story. Said he:

"At one time there was a great war among the animals, and one side had great difficulty in getting a commander who had sufficient confidence in himself. Finally they found a monkey by the name of Jocko, who said he thought he could command their army if his tail could be made a little longer. So they got more tail and spliced it on to his caudal appendage.

"He looked at it admiringly, and then he said he thought he ought to have still more tail. This was added, and again he called for more. The splicing process was repeated many times until they had coiled Jocko's tail around the room, filling all the space.

"Still he called for more tail, and, there being no other place to coil it, they began wrapping it around his shoulders. He continued his call for more, and they kept on winding the additional tail around him until its weight broke him down."

I saw the point, and, rising from my chair, replied,

"Mr. President, I will not call for any more assistance unless I find it impossible to do with what I already have."

AUTHORITY

The Chief Magistrate derives all his authority from the people.

—First Inaugural Address, March 4, 1861

AUTOGRAPH

One day President Lincoln received in the mail a request from a lady for an autograph and a "sentiment" with his signature. Annoyed by such a frivolous demand in the middle of a grave national crisis, Lincoln wrote in response:

"Dear Madam: When you ask from a stranger that which is of interest only to yourself, always enclose a stamp. There's your sentiment, and here's my autograph. A. Lincoln."

AVERAGE

The average man thinks he is better than average. President Lincoln was reminded of this fact when an old acquaintance paid a visit to him at the White House. Lincoln welcomed him warmly and even hoped to find a modest place for him in the government. However, the visitor, who was an honest man but utterly inexperienced in public affairs or finance, stunned the president by asking for one of the highest offices in the nation—superintendent of the Mint.

"Good gracious! Why didn't he ask to be secretary of the treasury and have done with it?" Lincoln mused later. "Well, now, I never thought Mr. Ludlow had anything more than average ability, when we were young men together. But, then, I suppose he thought the same thing about me, and—here I am!"

(see RESIGNATION)

AYES

When President Lincoln first met with his cabinet to present his proposed Emancipation Proclamation, he asked for a vote on the issue.

The cabinet voted overwhelmingly against it. After all the no votes had been counted, Lincoln raised his right hand and said, "The ayes have it!"

(see MINORITY)

B

BALDNESS

A bald, beardless congressman named John Ganson was a Democrat who supported Abraham Lincoln in Congress but demanded to be kept informed about every development on the front.

One day he visited the president at the White House to discuss the state of the Union. "Though I am a Democrat, I imperil my political future by supporting your war measures," said Ganson. "I can understand that secrecy may be necessary in military operations, but I think I am entitled to know the exact conditions, good or bad, at the front."

Lincoln looked at him for a moment or two and then exclaimed: "Ganson, how clean you shave!"

This remark ended the discussion. Ganson decided not to press the president further.

BALLOONIST

Abraham Lincoln told this story to illustrate how people sometimes jump to conclusions.

"A balloon ascension occurred in New Orleans before the war, and after sailing in the air for several hours the aeronaut, who was bedecked in silks and spangles like a circus performer, descended in a cotton field where a gang of slaves were at work.

"The frightened slaves, who had never seen anything like this before, took to the woods in haste—all but one venerable old man, who was rheumatic and could not run and who, seeing the resplendent balloonist, apparently having just dropped from heaven, hailed the strange visitor from the sky with the cry, "Good-mornin,' Massa Jesus; how's yo' pa?"

BANKERS

The secretary of the treasury, Hugh McCulloch, once introduced President Lincoln to a delegation of New York bankers. As they filed into the room, McCullough whispered to the president:

"These gentlemen from New York have come to see about our new loan. As bankers they are obliged to hold our national securities. I can vouch for their patriotism and loyalty, for, as the good Book says, 'Where the treasure is, there will the heart be also.' "

Lincoln nodded knowingly. "There is another text, Mr. McCulloch, I recall, that might equally apply. 'Where the carcass is there will the eagles be gathered together.' "

(see PROTECTION)

BARTENDER

During the Lincoln-Douglas debates, Illinois Senator Stephen A. Douglas tried to score a point by relating how when he first encountered Abraham Lincoln, the latter was a lowly storekeeper selling, among other things, whiskey and cigars. "Mr. Lincoln was a very good bartender!" exclaimed Douglas.

"What Mr. Douglas has said is true enough," Lincoln replied. "I did keep a grocery, and I did sell cotton, candles, and cigars, and sometimes whiskey. I remember in those days that Mr. Douglas was one of my best customers. Many a time have I stood on one side of the counter and sold whiskey to Mr. Douglas on the other side, but the difference between us now is this: I have left my side of the counter, but Mr. Douglas still sticks to his as tenaciously as ever."

(see DEBATE, HAT)

BEARD

Abraham Lincoln did not grow his famous beard until after he was nominated for the presidency in 1860. He was clean shaven until he received a letter from a little girl named Grace Bedell, who lived in Westfield, New York, saying she had seen his portrait and thought he would look better with whiskers. She promised that if he let his whiskers grow, she would try to persuade her older brothers, who were Democrats, to vote for him.

Lincoln wrote back to her on October 19, 1860:

"Miss Grace Bedell. My Dear Little Miss: Your very agreeable letter of the fifteenth is received. I regret the necessity of saying that I have no daughter. I have three sons: one seventeen, one nine, and one seven years of age. They, with their mother, constitute my whole family. As to the whiskers, having never worn any, do you not think people would call it a piece of silly affectation if I should begin it now? Your very sincere well-wisher, A. Lincoln.''

However, Lincoln soon changed his mind on the subject. When he was on his way to Washington to be inaugurated, the train stopped at Westfield. Remembering young Grace Bedell, Lincoln inquired after her. It was soon discovered that she was present in the crowd. The president-elect asked her to come forward so she might see that he had allowed his whiskers to grow at her request. She timidly obliged and he lifted her up and kissed her while the crowd roared its approval. He wore a beard ever after.

BIBLE

Take all of this book upon reason that you can, and the balance on faith, and you will live and die a happier and better man.

—Speed, *Reminiscences of Abraham Lincoln*
(see CHRISTIANITY, RELIGION)

BIG GOVERNMENT

Abraham Lincoln was wary of the unchecked growth of government. On one occasion, when a group of government officials approached President Lincoln with a petition to transfer control of certain funds to their federal hands, Lincoln offered this explanation of his denial of their request:

"You are very much like a man in Illinois whose cabin was burned down, and, according to the kindly custom of early days in the West, his neighbors all contributed something to start him again. In his case they were so liberal that he soon found himself better off than before the fire and got proud. One day a neighbor brought him a bag of oats, but the man refused it with scorn and said, 'I am not taking oats any more; now I take nothing but money.' "

(see GOVERNMENT)

BLACKS

In the right to eat the bread . . . which his own hand earns, he is my equal and the equal of Judge Douglas, and the equal of every living man.

—First joint debate with Stephen A. Douglas, August 21, 1858

All I ask for the Negro is that if you do not like him, let him alone.

—Speech to the Republican State Convention, July 17, 1858
(see DOUGLASS, SLAVERY)

BLAME

President Lincoln was interested in any peace proposal that allowed for the preservation of the Union. It did not matter to him which side was to blame for the war.

"Some of the supporters of the Union cause are opposed to accommodate or yield to the South in any manner or way because the Confederates began the war," said Lincoln. "Now this reminds me of a story I heard once, when I lived in Illinois.

"A vicious bull in a pasture took after everybody who tried to cross the lot, and one day a neighbor of the owner was the victim. This man was a speedy fellow and got to a friendly tree ahead of the bull, but not in time to climb the tree. So he led the enraged animal a merry race around the tree, finally succeeding in seizing the bull by the tail.

"The bull, being at a disadvantage, not able either to catch the man or to release his tail, was mad enough to eat nails; he dug up the earth with his feet, scattered gravel all around, bellowed until you could hear him for two miles or more, and at length broke into a dead run, the man hanging onto his tail all the time.

"While the bull, much out of temper, was legging it to the best of his ability, his tormentor, still clinging to the tail, demanded to know, 'Damn you, who commenced this fuss?' "

President Lincoln paused, then added: "It's our duty to settle this fuss at the earliest possible moment, no matter who commenced it, no matter who is to blame."

(see LEE)

BOOKS

Abraham Lincoln was a self-educated man who read and studied many books without the prompting of teachers. "The things I want to know are in books," he said. "My best friend is the man who'll get me a book I ain't read."

His formal schooling did not amount to more than a year altogether, but Lincoln was an avid reader outside the classroom. He read in the intervals of his farm work during the day and at night by firelight. His passion for politics was stirred by a borrowed copy of Weems's *Life of Washington*, and the discovery of a dusty edition of "The Statutes of Indiana" led to his lifelong interest in the law. But unquestionably Lincoln's two favorite books were the Bible and Aesop's Fables. Lincoln read both these works over and over; their lasting influence on him can be seen in his writing and his storytelling.

Dennis Hanks, one of Lincoln's cousins, observed that Lincoln derived more than other men from reading the same books. According to Hanks, "Abe made books tell him more than they told other people."

(see BIBLE, READING)

Books serve to show a man that those original thoughts of his aren't very new after all.

—Attributed

BOOTH, JOHN WILKES

John Wilkes Booth, a violent partisan of the Confederate cause, was the principal actor in a conspiracy to assassinate President Lincoln that involved twenty-five known individuals.

The conspirators also planned to assassinate Vice-president Andrew Johnson, Secretary of War Edwin M. Stanton, and General Ulysses S. Grant. Booth called on Vice-president Johnson the day before Lincoln's assassination, and not finding him at home, left a card. Booth also followed General Grant on several outings in the days before the assassination. General Grant had been invited to attend the theater with the Lincolns and had actually accepted the invitation; only a last-minute change of plans, instigated by Mrs. Grant, who wanted to visit their daughter in Burlington, Vermont, thwarted Booth's plan to kill both Lincoln and Grant at the same time.

After shooting Lincoln in the back of the head in the president's balcony box at Ford's Theater, Booth escaped from Washington on horseback and, accompanied by fellow conspirator David C. Herold, found refuge in a barn on Garrett's farm near Port Royal on the Rappahannock River in Maryland. Eleven days after the assassination Booth and Herold were cornered by a squad of cavalrymen, who surrounded the barn and demanded that the assassins surrender themselves. Herold gave himself up and was reviled by Booth, who vowed never to be taken alive.

The cavalrymen then set fire to the barn in an effort to drive Booth out. When the flames first flared up, Booth crawled forward on his hands and knees, apparently with the intention of shooting the man who had applied the torch, but the smoke and the blaze soon blinded him. As the flames soared skyward, the figure of Booth could be seen, standing upright on a crutch, holding a carbine in his hands, but he could not see his pursuers. Realizing any attempt to extinguish the fire was futile, Booth limped toward the door with his carbine ready.

Wearing the uniform of a Confederate soldier, he was pale, haggard, and unkempt. He had shaved off his mustache and cut his hair short.

The cavalrymen were under orders not to shoot Booth. "Take him alive!" they had been told. But these orders were disobeyed by a sergeant known as "Boston" Corbett, who fired through a crevice in the barn and hit Booth in the neck. The wounded assassin was carried out of the barn and laid in the grass. "Tell mother I died for my country," he whispered just before he died. "I thought I did for the best."

No one knows what became of Booth's body. It was taken to Washington where a postmortem was held on the Monitor Montauk. Then on the evening of April 27 it was turned over to two men who took it in a rowboat and disposed of it secretly.

Four of Booth's coconspirators—David Herold, G. W. Atzerodt, Samuel Arnold, and Mrs. Mary Surratt (whose boardinghouse had been used as a meeting place for the conspirators)—were hanged.

A successful actor by trade, noted for his Shakespearean roles, John Wilkes Booth (1838-65) was the son of the well-known Anglo-American actor Junius Brutus Booth (1796–1852) and the younger brother of the actor Edwin Thomas Booth (1833–93), who retired from the stage after John's disgrace but later came out of retirement to become one of the most highly acclaimed tragic actors in the history of the American stage.

(see ASSASSINATION, DEATH,
KENNEDY ASSASSINATION PARALLELS)

BORE

Bores are attracted to power like moths to a light. No president can be completely protected from harassment by bores. A bald-headed Philadelphia man who was an infamous bore encroached so persistently on the president's time that Abraham Lincoln had to contrive a clever ruse to get rid of him.

On this particular day many delegations were waiting to see the president, but the bald-headed bore lingered long and babbled on and on. Finally Lincoln walked over to a wardrobe in the corner of the cabinet chamber, with the Philadelphia man tagging along and talking fast. Taking down a bottle from the shelf, Lincoln asked the man:

"Did you ever try this stuff for your hair?"

"No, sir, I never did."

"Well, I advise you to try it. Here, I will give you this bottle. If at first you don't succeed, try, try again. Keep it up. They say it will make hair grow on a pumpkin. Now take it and come back in eight or ten months and tell me how it works."

The man took the bottle and left without further comment.

(see COUNSELORS)

BOYS

One of nature's timeless truths—and parenthood's lesser joys—is that boys will be boys. President Lincoln was a doting father, who frequently allowed his young son, "Tad," to accompany him on business. Once, on a trip to Fortress Monroe, Tad tried his father's patience. President Lincoln, who was trying to talk with one of his grown-up companions, offered Tad an inducement to good behavior. "Tad," he said, "if you will be a good boy and not disturb me any more until we get to Fortress Monroe, I will give you a dollar."

This incentive was sufficient to silence Tad for a while, until his boyishness got the better of him and, forgetting his promise, he was as noisy as before. Upon arrival at Fortress Monroe, however, Tad tugged on his father's sleeve and said, "I want my dollar."

Lincoln looked at the lad half-reproachfully, then pulled a dollar from his billfold, saying: "Well, my son, at any rate, I will keep my half of the bargain."

(see SHARING)

BRAGGING

Nothing was more irritating to President Lincoln than the bragging of generals about what they would do if they ever met the enemy face to face. In their performance on the battlefield they rarely lived up to their bold, boastful predictions.

Hearing that one such general had been soundly beaten in the field by the Confederates, President Lincoln sighed and said,

"It reminds me of the fellow who owned a dog that, so he said, just hungered and thirsted to combat and eat up wolves. It was a difficult matter, so the owner declared, to keep that dog from devoting the entire twenty-four hours of each day to the destruction of his enemies. He just 'hankered' to get at them.

"One day a party of this dog owner's friends thought to have some sport. These friends heartily disliked wolves and were anxious to see the dog eat up a few thousand. So they organized a hunting party and invited the dog owner and the dog to go with them. They desired to be personally present when the wanton slaughter of the wolves was in progress.

"It was noticed that the dog owner was not overenthusiastic in the matter; he pleaded a 'business engagement,' but as he was the most notorious and torpid of the town loafers and wouldn't have recognized a 'business engagement' had he met it face to face, his excuse was treated with contempt. Therefore he had to go.

"The dog, however, was glad enough to go, and so the party started out. Wolves were in plenty, and soon a pack was discovered, but when the 'wolf-hound' saw the ferocious animals, he lost heart, and, putting his tail between his legs, endeavored to slink away. At last, after many trials, he was enticed into the small growth of underbrush where the wolves had secreted themselves, and yelps of terror betrayed the fact that the battle was on.

"Away flew the wolves, the dog among them, the hunting party following on horseback. The wolves seemed frightened, and the dog was restored to public favor. It really looked as if he had the savage creatures on the run, since he was fighting heroically when last sighted.

"Wolves and dog soon disappeared, and it was not until the party arrived at a distant farmhouse that news of the combatants was gleaned.

" 'Have you seen anything of a wolf-dog and a pack of wolves around here?' was the question anxiously put to the male occupant of the house, who stood idly leaning upon the gate.

" 'Yep,' was the short answer.

" 'How were they going?'

" 'Purty fast.'

" 'What was their position when you saw them?'
" 'Well,' replied the farmer, in a most exasperatingly
deliberate way, 'the dog was a leetle bit ahead.'

"Now, gentleman," President Lincoln concluded,
"that's the position in which you'll find most of these
bragging generals when they get into a fight with the
enemy. That's why I don't like military orators."

(see RUNNING)

BRAVERY

No one can succeed all alone. Even the bravest heroes
need help from time to time. To illustrate this fact, Abraham Lincoln told the following story:

"Back in the early days, a hunting party went out to
track a wild boar. But the game came upon them unexpectedly, and they all scrambled toward the treetops, all
save one, the bravest hunter of them all, who, seizing
the animal by the ears, undertook to hold the beast.
After holding it for some time and finding his strength
giving way, the hero cried out to his companions in the
trees:

" 'Boys, come down and help me let go!' "

BREVITY

Lawyers are not known for their brevity, and lawyers'
briefs are rarely brief. Remarking on a particularly long
brief written by a wordy lawyer, Abraham Lincoln said,
"It's like the lazy preacher who used to write long sermons, and the explanation was, he got to writin' and
was too lazy to stop."

(see WORDS)

BULL RUN

After the battle of Bull Run, President Lincoln heard some accounts of the conflict that reflected more favorably on the Union cause than events would warrant.

Listening to one such report, President Lincoln raised one eyebrow and asked, "So, it is your notion that we whipped the rebels and then ran away from them?"

(see RUNNING)

C

CABINET

President Lincoln filled his cabinet with prominent men, some of them former rivals who considered themselves equal or superior to the president.

A few weeks after the 1860 election, when the first appointments were announced, a Springfield, Illinois, banker named John Bunn bumped into Senator Salmon Chase coming out of Lincoln's law office in Springfield.

"Surely you don't want to put that man in your cabinet," said Bunn as soon as Chase was gone.

"Why not?" asked Lincoln.

"Because," said Bunn, "he thinks he is a great deal bigger than you are."

"Well, do you know of any other men who think they are bigger than I am?" Lincoln wanted to know.

"I don't know that I do," said Bunn. "Why do you ask?"

"Because," Lincoln replied, "I want to put them all in my cabinet."

(see PAPER MONEY SKUNKS)

CAPITAL

Capital has its rights, which are as worthy of protection as any other rights.

—Annual Message to Congress, December 3, 1861
(see LABOR, PROPERTY)

CAPITALISTS

A few men own capital, and that few avoid labor themselves.

—Annual Message to Congress, 1861

These capitalists generally act harmoniously, and in concert, to fleece the people.

—Address to the Illinois legislature, January 11, 1837
(see LABOR, PROPERTY)

CAPITAL PUNISHMENT

During the Civil War, President Lincoln granted pardons to many Union soldiers who had been given death sentences by military courts. But he was not unconditionally opposed to capital punishment. For example, he refused to lift the death sentences assigned to five convicted "bounty jumpers"—men who were paid by localities for enlisting and who then deserted after receiving their bounties.

Although he was often criticized for granting too many pardons, President Lincoln was responsible for ordering the largest mass hanging in American history—thirty-eight Sioux Indians on December 26, 1862.

This tragic turn of events began in the summer of 1862 when starving Sioux Indians, furious about broken promises from the federal government, attacked several small settlements in Minnesota.

Most of the able-bodied men were off fighting in the Civil War, which left the towns vulnerable to attack. In the bloodiest of all the Indian massacres, at least eight hundred settlers were killed. The Indians quickly seized control of a 250-by-50-mile strip of land. Eventually, however, the Indian uprising was subdued by U.S. army troops under the command of General John Pope. Hundreds of Sioux were imprisoned in the military stockade.

A military tribunal was established and, after a hasty hearing, 307 Sioux warriors were condemned to die. But there were questions about the legal authority of the tribunal, and ultimately the matter was dumped in Lincoln's lap.

President Lincoln, as commander in chief, personally reviewed each of the 307 cases. Then he wrote an order for the execution of the 38 Sioux he judged to be clearly guilty of murdering unarmed citizens—commuting the death sentences of the rest.

A huge scaffold, twenty-four feet square, was constructed in Mankato, Minnesota, for the public hanging. On the morning of December 26, the condemned Indians mounted the scaffold. Ropes were looped about their necks, and as the platform gave way beneath their feet, a crowd of four thousand civilians cheered.

The ordering of this execution was one of Lincoln's least glorious achievements, and one that historians often whitewash, but it illustrates the hard decisions he had to make daily as president during the Civil War.

(see PARDONS)

CAPTIVES

When President Lincoln was informed that the Confederates had captured a brigadier general and twelve army mules, he was saddened by the news. "How unfortunate!" he said, heaving a heavy sigh. "Those *mules* cost us two hundred dollars apiece!"

(see GENERALS)

CAUSE AND EFFECT

The laws of cause and effect apply to the political world, as well as to the physical world.

A citizen of Springfield, Illinois, once asked Abraham Lincoln what attribute he considered most valuable to the successful politician.

Lincoln's reply was thought-provoking, even profound: "To be able to raise a cause which shall produce an effect, and then *fight the effect*."

CHARACTER

Character is like a tree and reputation like its shadow. The shadow is what we think of it; the tree is the real thing.

—Gross, *Lincoln's Own Stories*, p. 109

CHARITY

"Give to him that is needy" is the Christian rule of charity; but "Take from him that is needy" is the rule of slavery.

—On Pro-Slavery Theology, October 1, 1858
from fragment "Pro-Slavery Theology"
October 1, 1858 (date approximate)
(see SLAVERY)

CHILDREN

Love is the chain whereby to bind a child to his parents.

—Carpenter, *Six Months at the White House*, 1866

CHRISTIANITY

People are inclined to judge a religion not by its founder but by its representatives. To illustrate this point, Abraham Lincoln told a story about an old-line Baptist preacher who rose in the pulpit one Sunday and announced his text with the words: "I am the Christ whom I shall represent today."

The preacher was dressed in coarse linen pantaloons and a tow linen shirt. The pants were made, in the old fashioned way, with baggy legs and a flap in the front, attaching to his frame without the aid of suspenders.

Just as the preacher was commencing his sermon, a little blue lizard darted into his roomy pantaloons. Not wishing to interrupt his eloquent appeal to the souls of his parishioners, the preacher slapped his leg while he talked, hoping to stop the invader, but his efforts did not avail, and the varmint climbed higher and higher.

The preacher loosened the central button on the waistband of his pantaloons as he spoke, and with a kick, he dropped that loose-fitting garment to the floor. But by this time the lizard had passed the equator of the waistband and was exploring the part of the preacher's anatomy that lay underneath the back of his shirt.

Still the sermon did not cease. The preacher's next movement, in the attempt to liberate himself from the annoying lizard, was to undo the collar button, and with one impatient sweep of his arm, he took off his tow linen shirt.

The congregation sat in silence for a few moments as if stunned; finally, an elderly lady in the rear of the one-room meetinghouse rose, and glaring at the excited object in the pulpit, announced at the top of her lungs: "If you represent Christ, then I'm done with the Bible!"

(see BIBLE, GOD, RELIGION)

CIVIL WAR

It is a struggle for maintaining in the world that form and substance of government whose leading object is to elevate the condition of men—to lift artificial weights from all shoulders—to clear the paths of laudable pursuit for all—to afford all an unfettered start, and a fair chance, in the race of life.

—Message to Congress in a special session, July 4, 1861

Both read the same Bible and pray to the same God, and each invokes His aid against the other. It may seem strange that any men should dare to ask a just God's assistance in wringing their bread from the sweat of other men's faces.

—Second Inaugural Address, March 4, 1865

Fondly do we hope, fervently do we pray, that this mighty scourge of war may speedily pass away. Yet, if God wills that this continue until all the wealth piled by the bondsman's two hundred and fifty years of unrequited toil shall be sunk, and until every drop of blood drawn with the lash shall be paid by another drawn with the sword, as was said three thousand years ago, so still it must be said, "The judgments of the Lord are true and righteous altogether."

—Second Inaugural Address, March 4, 1865
(see AMERICA, CONFEDERATES, GENERALS, PRAYER, UNION, ETC.)

CLASSES

The habits of our whole species fall into three great classes—useful labor, useless labor and idleness. Of these the first only is meritorious; and to it all the products of labor rightfully belong; but the latter two, while they exist, are heavy pensioners upon the first, robbing it of a large portion of its rights.

—Fragment of a tariff discussion, December 1, 1847
(see LABOR, MARX)

COFFEE

If this is coffee, please bring me some tea; but if this is tea, please bring me some coffee.

—Attributed, a remark to a hotel waiter

COLDS

A congressman called at the White House one day and found the president suffering from a bad cold. When the congressman conveyed his sympathy, Lincoln pointed down at his uncommonly large feet and said self-deprecatingly, "I expect colds. There's so much of me on the ground, you see."

(see FEET)

COMMAND

Abraham Lincoln was elected captain of a group of volunteers to fight in the Black Hawk Indian War. Inexperienced in the formalities of military drill and maneuvering, he made many mistakes when issuing his commands. But his native ingenuity usually enabled him to extricate himself from difficulties. One time, when Lincoln was marching in front of a squad of twenty men, he found the path blocked by a narrow gate that offered passage for only one person into the next field.

"For the life of me I could not remember the proper word of command for getting my company endwise so that it could get through the gate. So as we came near I said, 'This company is dismissed for two minutes, when it will fall in again on the other side of the gate.' "

COMMON MAN

God must love the common man, he made so many of them.

—Attributed
(see PEOPLE)

COMPENSATION

This is a world of compensation; and he who would be no slave must consent to have no slave. Those who deny freedom to others deserve it not for themselves, and, under a just God, cannot long retain it.

—Letter to H. L. Pierce and others, April 6, 1859
(see SLAVERY)

CONFEDERATES

At a cabinet meeting, someone asked how many men the Confederates had in the field.

"Twelve hundred thousand, according to the best authority," declared President Lincoln.

"Good Heavens!" The room resounded with exclamations of alarm.

"Yes, sir," repeated Lincoln, "twelve hundred thousand—no doubt about it. You see, all our generals, when they get whipped, say the enemy outnumbers them four to one, and I must believe them. We have four hundred thousand men in the field, and three times that makes twelve hundred thousand, don't you see?"

(see EXAGGERATION)

Why, gentlemen, I think you are as gallant and as brave men as live; that you can fight as bravely in a good cause, man for man, as any other people living . . . but, man for man, you are not better than we are, and there are not so many of you as there are of us. . . . If we were fewer in numbers than you, I think you could whip us; if we were equal, it would likely be a drawn battle; but, being inferior in numbers, you will make nothing by attempting to master us. . . . We intend in the end to beat you.

—Speech to Confederates in Cincinnati, 1859
(see DOG, ENEMIES, VICTORY)

CONGRESS

When he was running for Congress in 1846, Abraham Lincoln attended a preaching service by Peter Cartwright, known for his sermons against the sins of drinking, gambling, and wearing ruffles. Toward the end of the service Cartwright called on all who wanted to go to heaven to stand up. All arose but Lincoln. Then Cartwright asked all to rise who did not want to go to hell. Again Lincoln was the only one to remain seated.

"I am surprised to see Abe Lincoln sitting back there unmoved by these appeals," said Cartwright. "If Mr. Lincoln does not want to go to heaven and does not plan to escape hell, perhaps he will tell us where he does want to go."

Lincoln rose. "I am going to Congress."

(see SAMENESS)

CONSCIENCE

I desire so to conduct the affairs of this administration that if at the end, when I come to lay down the reins of power, I have lost every other friend on earth, I shall at least have one friend left, and that friend shall be down inside me.

—Reply to the Missouri Committee of Seventy, 1864
(see GOD, INTEGRITY)

CONSERVATISM

What is conservatism? Is it not adherence to the old and tried, against the new and untried?

—Address, Cooper Union, New York, February 27, 1860
(see OPEN-MINDEDNESS, PAST)

CONTROL

I claim not to have controlled events, but confess plainly that events have controlled me.

—Letter to A. G. Hodges, April 4, 1864

CORPSES

A sensitive man who was raised by Quakers and loathed violence, Abraham Lincoln in his lifetime saw more than one man's share of bloodshed. He never forgot the first time he saw corpses on the field. It was during the Black Hawk Indian War, in the vicinity of the skirmish at Kellogg's Grove in Illinois. Coming up a slope toward a campsite at sunrise, Lincoln found that the men had been slaughtered in their sleep.

Lincoln later informed his biographer Noah Brooks—the Civil War correspondent who wrote *The Life of Lincoln*—that he still "remembered just how those men looked as we rode up the little hill where their camp was. The red light of the morning sun was streaming upon them as they lay, heads toward us, on the ground. And every man had a round, red spot on the top of his head about as big as a dollar, where the redskins had taken his scalp. It was frightful, but it was grotesque; and the red sunlight seemed to paint everything all over."

Recollecting the grisly scene, delineated with the irrelevant details so often characteristic of human memory, he added: "I remember that one man had on buckskin breeches."

(see HOG)

COUNSELORS

President Lincoln was afflicted with the voluble advice of a great many counselors who were all too eager to tell him how to run the country and how to win the Civil War. Sometimes this advice was firsthand, sometimes secondhand; sometimes from the living, sometimes from the dead.

After returning from a trip to Washington, Peter Harvey, the pompous friend and biographer of the deceased Daniel Webster, was asked his impression of President Lincoln.

"Mr. Lincoln is a very singular man," replied Harvey. "I went in to see him and informed him that I'd been an intimate personal friend of Daniel Webster and that I felt perfectly competent to tell him what Mr. Webster would advise in the present crisis; whereupon I talked to Mr. Lincoln for two solid hours, telling him precisely what he should do and what he should not do, in Mr. Webster's view, and—would you believe it?—when I got through, all Mr. Lincoln said was, as he clapped his

hand on my leg, 'Mr. Harvey, what tremendous great
calves you have got!' "

(see BORE)

COURTESY

At the end of the Civil War, when the Confederate capital of Richmond was evacuated by the rebel troops,
President Lincoln walked through the city in triumph.
At one point during the informal parade, an old black
man approached, removed his hat, bowed respectfully,
and said, "May de good Lord bless you, President
Linkum."

President Lincoln took off his own top hat and bowed
respectfully in return.

(see DOUGLASS)

COURT-MARTIAL

One of the most highly publicized court-martial cases
during the Civil War was that of Franklin W. Smith and
his brother Benjamin G. Smith of Boston, charged with
defrauding the government. In this troubled time,
courts-martial were seldom staged for any other purpose than to convict the accused, and although the
Smiths bore a reputation for high integrity, they shared
the usual fate. They were imprisoned, their papers were
seized, their businesses were closed, their reputations
were ruined, and they were convicted.

The finding of the court was submitted to the commander in chief. After a careful investigation, President
Lincoln disapproved the judgment and wrote:

"Whereas, Franklin W. Smith had transactions with
the Navy Department to the amount of a million and
quarter of dollars; and

"Whereas he had a chance to steal at least a quarter of a million and was only charged with stealing twenty-two hundred dollars and the question is now about his stealing one hundred, I don't believe he stole anything at all.

"Therefore, the record and findings are disapproved, declared null and void and the defendants are fully discharged."

(see HANDSOME, PARDON, REPRIEVE)

COWS

President Lincoln butted heads on many occasions with General George B. McClellan, who eventually ran against him for president in 1864. When McClellan was commander of the Union forces, Lincoln demanded that the general report to him frequently, and McClellan resented it. The general once sent Lincoln the following telegram from the field:

President Abraham Lincoln
Washington, D.C.

Have just captured six cows. What shall we do with them?

—George B. McClellan

Lincoln immediately wired back:

General George B. McClellan
Army of the Potomac

Milk them.
    —A. Lincoln

(see MCCLELLAN)

COWARDICE

To sin by silence when they should protest makes cowards of men.

—Attributed

CREDITOR

It was Abraham Lincoln's practice to discourage unnecessary lawsuits, even though this policy cost him business as a lawyer. But Lincoln learned that some people go to court not so much to win their rights as to be proved right. On one occasion a man who asked him to bring suit for a debt of $2.50 would not be dissuaded from suing. Lincoln therefore demanded $10 dollars as a retainer. His client paid him the $10. Lincoln gave half this amount to the indigent defendant, who confessed the judgment and paid the $2.50. Thus the suit was resolved to the satisfaction of the creditor.

(see LAWSUITS)

CRISIS

If there ever could be a proper time for mere catch arguments, that time surely is not now. In times like the present, men should utter nothing for which they would not willingly be responsible through time and eternity.

—Second Annual Message to Congress,
December 1, 1862
(see ARGUMENT)

CRITICS

Once when President Lincoln heard his administration harshly criticized at a convention he said, "Ladies and gentlemen, suppose all the property you were worth was in gold, and you had put it in the hands of Blondin [the French highwire artist who walked across the Niagara River three times in 1855, 1859, and 1860] to carry across the Niagara River on a rope. Would you shake the cable and keep shouting—'Blondin, stoop a little more—go a little faster—lean a little more to the left—to the right—to the north—to the south?' No, you would hold your breath as well as your tongue, and keep your hands off until he was safe over. This government is carrying an immense weight. Untold treasures are in our hands. We are doing the very best we can. Don't badger us. Keep quiet, and we will get you safe across.''

(see EDITORIALS)

If I were to try to read, much less answer, all the attacks on me, this shop might as well be closed for any other business. I do the very best I know how—the very best I can; and I mean to keep doing so until the end. If the end brings me out all right, what is said against me won't amount to anything. If the end brings me out wrong, ten angels swearing I was right would make no difference.

—Carpenter, Six Months at the White House, 1866

CUSTOM

During a trial, Abraham Lincoln's adversary argued that custom legalized all things and precedent took precedence over law.

Lincoln countered this argument with a story that describes a type of rural character common in those times:

"Old Squire Bagley, from Menard, came into my office one day and said:

" 'Lincoln, I want your advice as a lawyer. Has a man

what's been elected justice of the peace a right to issue a marriage license?'

"I told him no, whereupon the old squire threw himself back in his chair very indignantly, shook his head, and said:

" 'Lincoln, I thought you was a lawyer. Now, Bob Thomas and me had a bet on this thing, and we agreed to let you decide; but if this is your opinion I don't want it, for I know a thunderin' sight better. You're wrong. I've been a squire eight years, and I've issued marriage licenses all the time.' "

D

DANCING

When awkward young Abraham Lincoln was a suitor to Mary Todd, he approached her at a party and said, "Miss Todd, I should like to dance with you in the worst way."

After she negotiated a few clumsy circuits of the room with this tall, ungainly man, she was deposited back in her seat, surrounded by her giggling girlfriends.

"Well, Mary, did he dance with you the worst way?" asked one.

"Yes," replied Mary Todd, "the worst way."

(see BIOGRAPHY 1842)

DAVIS, JEFFERSON

Jefferson Davis, the president of the Confederacy, insisted on being addressed by his official title as commander or president in the regular negotiations with the

U.S. government. But President Lincoln refused to oblige.

One of Davis's envoys, Mr. Hunt, cited the correspondence between King Charles I and his Parliament as a precedent for a negotiation between a constitutional ruler and rebels.

Appalled by the analogy, President Lincoln gazed at Hunt for a moment, then replied coolly: "Upon questions of history, I must refer you to Mr. Seward, for he is posted in such things, and I don't profess to be; but my only distinct recollection of the matter is that Charles lost his head."

(see TITLES)

DEATH

President Lincoln's last day was Good Friday, April 14, 1865. It was only five days after the surrender of Robert E. Lee, and it seemed that the long national nightmare was over.

Rising early as usual, Lincoln was in his office by seven. During the morning he met with General Ulysses S. Grant, who gave him details of the surrender, and then he met with his cabinet. He urged that there should be no persecutions, for too much blood had already been shed.

After lunch Lincoln signed a pardon for a deserter who had been sentenced to be shot. "I think the boy can do us more good above the ground than under the ground," he said. He also revoked the death sentence of a Confederate spy. Next he held an interview with Nancy Bushrod, a black woman who came to the White House to ask for his help. She and her husband Tom had been slaves in Virginia until the Emancipation Proclamation, after which they moved to Washington. Tom joined the army, leaving her with their three children. At first his army pay came to her, but then inexplicably it ceased coming. She had searched unsuccessfully for employment and now was desperate.

"You are entitled to your soldier-husband's pay," Lincoln told her. "Come this time tomorrow and the papers will be signed and ready for you."

Tears filled her eyes. She smiled, and turned to leave.

"My good woman," Lincoln called to her, "perhaps you'll see many a day when all the food in the house is a single loaf of bread. Even so, give every child a slice and send your children off to school."

Then Lincoln bowed to her—"lak I wuz a natchral bawn lady," she said later—a gesture she never forgot.

At four in the afternoon, Lincoln left his office for a quiet drive with Mrs. Lincoln. "We must *both* be more cheerful in the future," he resolved. "Between the war and the loss of our darling Willie, we have both been very miserable."

Lincoln was not anxious to go to the theater that night to see *Our American Cousin*, which he had seen before, but Mrs. Lincoln had her heart set on it, and he had promised to attend. "It has been advertised that we will be there," Lincoln remarked to White House guard Colonel William Crook, "and I cannot disappoint the people. Otherwise I would not go. I do not want to go."

As he left the White House Lincoln said, "Goodbye, Crook."

This comment perplexed the colonel, for the president usually said, "Goodnight."

Lincoln entered Ford's Theater fifteen minutes late, with his wife and their friends, Major H. R. Rathbone and his fiancée Clara. The performance stopped. The crowd cheered as Lincoln entered the box. He waved and sat down in a haircloth rocking chair in the back of the box. A guard assigned to protect him found a seat so he could watch the play.

During the third act, Mrs. Lincoln reached out to hold her husband's hand. A shot was heard. Mrs. Lincoln screamed. John Wilkes Booth jumped to the stage shouting *"Sic semper tyrannis"* (the motto of Virginia, meaning "thus always to tyrants") and then escaped from the theater.

Lincoln was carried across the street to the home of William Peterson, a tailor, where he clung to life through the night and died the next morning at 7:22 A.M.

"Now he belongs to the ages," declared Secretary of War Edwin M. Stanton.

(see ASSASSINATION, BOOTH,
KENNEDY ASSASSINATION PARALLELS)

The death of the late president may not be without its use, in reminding us that *we*, too, must die. Death, abstractly considered, is the same with the high as with the low; but practically, we are not so much aroused to the contemplation of our own mortal natures by the fall of *many* undistinguished, as that of *one* great and well-known name. By the latter, we are forced to muse, and ponder, sadly.

—On the death of Zachary Taylor, July 25, 1850

DEBATE

"I can recall only one fact of the debates," wrote Mrs. William Crotty of Seneca, Illinois, who witnessed several of the famous debates between Abraham Lincoln and Stephen A. Douglas, "that I felt so sorry for Lincoln while Douglas was speaking, and then to my surprise I felt so sorry for Douglas when Lincoln replied."

(see BARTENDER)

When I'm getting ready to reason with a man, I spend about one-third of my time thinking about myself and what I am going to say—and two-thirds thinking about him and what he is going to say.

—Attributed

DECLARATION OF INDEPENDENCE

I have never had a feeling, politically, that did not spring from the sentiments embodied in the Declaration of Independence. . . . I have often inquired of myself what great principle or idea it was that kept this Confederacy so long together. It was not the mere matter of separation of the colonies from the motherland, but that sentiment in the Declaration of Independence which gave liberty not alone to the people of this country, but hope to all the world, for all future time. It was that which gave promise that in due time the weights would be lifted from the shoulders of all men, and that all should have an equal chance. This is the sentiment embodied in the Declaration of Independence. . . . I would rather be assassinated on this spot than surrender it.

—Speech at Independence Hall, Philadelphia,
February 22, 1861
(see AMERICA, LIBERTY, SLAVERY)

DEFEAT

Abraham Lincoln kept his sense of humor in defeat, which made him seem undefeated and, in a way, unbeatable. After he lost to Stephen A. Douglas in the Illinois Senate race in 1858, Lincoln was asked how he felt about this setback. He answered, "I feel somewhat like the boy in Kentucky who stubbed his toe while running to see his sweetheart. The boy said he was too big to cry, and far too badly hurt to laugh."

Despite this defeat, Lincoln refused to lower his aspirations. "I have an abiding faith," he wrote to an old friend on December 12, 1858, "that we shall beat them in the long run."

Two years later, Abraham Lincoln was elected president of the United States.

(see AMBITION, FAILURE)

DEMOCRACY

"Government of the people, by the people, for the people," Abraham Lincoln's immortal definition of democracy, was not wholly original when he gave it proverbial form in the Gettysburg Address. The idea had been expressed earlier in slightly different phrases by such well-known patriots as Daniel Webster, William Lloyd Garrison, and Theodore Parker. But Lincoln expressed it best.

. . . we here highly resolve that these dead shall not have died in vain; that this nation, under God, shall have a new birth of freedom; and that government of the people, by the people, for the people, shall not perish from the earth.

—Gettysburg Address, November 19, 1863

I go for all sharing the privileges of the government who assist in bearing its burdens.

—Letter to the Editor, *Sangamo Journal*, New Salem, Illinois, June 13, 1836

As I would not be a *slave*, so I would not be a *master*. This expresses my idea of democracy. Whatever differs from this, to the extent of the difference, is no democracy.

—Fragment found on a scrap of paper, August 1, 1858
(see GOVERNMENT, PEOPLE, SLAVERY)

DIGNITY

Abraham Lincoln got cold feet and failed to show up for his wedding to Mary Todd the first time it was scheduled, but the second attempt, on November 4, 1842, was more successful. An Episcopal church service was conducted, presided over by Reverend Charles Dresser.

When Lincoln placed the wedding ring on his bride's finger, he said, "With this ring I now thee wed, and with all my worldly goods I thee endow."

"Good God, Lincoln," remarked Judge Thomas Browne, who was present at the occasion. "The statute fixes all that."

Lincoln smiled benignly. "I just thought I'd add a little dignity to the statute."

(see BIOGRAPHY 1842)

DISCREDIT

When he was a young lawyer in Illinois, Abraham Lincoln was once charged by a certain Major Hill with making defamatory remarks about Mrs. Hill.

Major Hill heaped abuse on Lincoln in front of several witnesses, while Lincoln coolly kept his temper. Finally, when Lincoln had an opportunity to get a word in edgewise, he replied, "I have always had the highest regard for Mrs. Hill and I never made any of the remarks you have attributed to me. Mrs. Hill is a fine woman and the only thing I know to her discredit is the fact that she is Major Hill's wife."

(see JURORS)

DISCRETION

When you have got an elephant by the hind leg and he
is trying to run away, it's best to let him run.

—Remark to Charles Dana on April 14, 1865
(Lincoln's last known aphorism)

DIVORCES

Military matters were muddled during the period when
President Lincoln, unhappy with General George B.
McClellan's performance as Union commander, began considering removing him and replacing him
with another general. McClellan's supporters threatened to go over to the Democratic party if Lincoln
fired their man. Meanwhile the Confederate armies
marched in circles around the stationary General Mc-
Clellan.

"This situation reminds me," mused Lincoln at a cabinet meeting shortly before the appointment of General
Henry W. Halleck as McClellan's successor as Union
Commander in Chief, "of a Union man in Kentucky
whose two sons enlisted in the Union army. His wife
was of Confederate sympathies. His nearest neighbor
was a Confederate in feeling, and his two sons were
fighting under Lee. But this neighbor's wife was a Union
woman and it nearly broke her heart to know that her
sons were arrayed against the Union.

"Finally, the two men, after each had talked matters
over with his wife, agreed to obtain divorces; this they
did, and then they swapped wives. The Union man and
the Union woman were wedded, as were the Confederate man and the Confederate woman. But this didn't
seem to help matters much, for the sons of the Union
woman were still fighting for the South, and the sons
of the Confederate woman continued fighting in the

Union cause; the Union husband couldn't get along with his Union wife, and the Confederate husband and his Confederate wife couldn't agree upon anything, being forever fussing and quarreling.

"It's the same thing with the army," Lincoln concluded. He decided to allow McClellan to retain command of the Army of the Potomac, reflecting, "It doesn't seem worthwhile to secure divorces and then marry the army and McClellan to others, for they won't get along any better than they do now, and there'll only be a new set of heartaches started. I think we'd better wait; perhaps a real fighting general will come along one of these days, and then we'll all be happy. If you go to mixing in a mix-up, you only make the muddle worse."

(see COWS, MCCLELLAN)

DIXIE

General Robert E. Lee's surrender at Appomattox on April 9, 1865, spurred a series of celebrations in Washington. A brass band, followed by a crowd of over three thousand people, marched to the White House.

President Lincoln came out to greet them. He read some remarks he had written that day to commemorate the occasion. As he finished reading each page of his speech, he let it drop to the ground, and his son Tad picked it up.

"Give me another paper!" cried Tad, much to the amusement of the audience.

At the conclusion of his address, Lincoln said, "I propose closing up this interview by having the band perform a particular tune which I will name. Before this is done, however, I wish to mention one or two little circumstances connected with it. I have always thought

'Dixie' one of the best tunes I ever heard. Our adversaries over the way attempted to appropriate it, but I insisted yesterday that we fairly captured it. I presented the question to the attorney-general, and he gave it as his legal opinion that it is our lawful prize. I now request the band to favor me with its performance."

The band then played "Dixie."

(see BIOGRAPHY 1865)

DOG

When the Confederate army of General John B. Hood was broken up into fragments along the border of Tennessee, President Lincoln was elated at the defeat of what had been for a long time a fierce and menacing threat to the Union army.

"It reminds me of the fate of a savage dog that belonged to one of my neighbors in the frontier settlements of Kentucky where I lived as boy. The dog was the terror of the neighborhood, and its owner, a churlish and quarrelsome fellow, took pleasure in the brute's forcible attitude and the fear it inspired.

"Finally, all other means having failed to subdue the creature, a man who particularly loathed the dog loaded a lump of meat with a charge of gunpowder, to which was attached a slow fuse; this was dropped where the dreaded dog would be sure to find it, and sure enough, the dog gulped down the tempting bait.

"Shortly afterward, there was a dull rumbling, a muffled explosion, and fragments of the dog were seen flying in every direction. It rained pieces of that pugnacious dog for ten minutes. The grieved owner, gathering together what fragments of his favorite he could find, said with sad resignation, 'He was a good dog, but as a dog, his days of usefulness are over.'

"Well, Hood's army was a good army," said Lincoln,

"and we were all afraid of it, but as an army, its days of usefulness are over."

(see CONFEDERATES)

DOUGLAS, STEPHEN A.

They have seen in his round, jolly, fruitful face, post-offices, land-offices, marshal-ships and cabinet-appointments, charge-ships and foreign missions, bursting out in wonderful exuberance.

—Speech against Stephen A. Douglas
in the campaign of 1860
(see DEBATE, HAT)

DOUGLASS, FREDERICK

Hearing that Frederick Douglass, the great black abolitionist, was visiting Washington, President Lincoln invited him to the White House for tea. Recalling the occasion, Douglass commented, "Lincoln is the first white man I ever spent an hour with who did not remind me that I am a Negro."

(see BLACKS, COURTESY)

DRAFT

This is the story of Abraham Lincoln's last laugh. On April 13, 1865, the Civil War being ended at last, Lincoln ordered an end to the drafting of soldiers. The following night, during the fateful performance of *Our American Cousin* at Ford's Theater in Washington, there was a scene in which the heroine of the play, reclining on a garden seat, called for a shawl to protect her from the draft.

The actor to whom the request was addressed, Edward Sothern, replied with an ad-lib line: "You are mistaken, Miss Mary, the draft has already been stopped by order of the president!"

Abraham Lincoln laughed heartily, along with the rest of the audience, at this impromptu joke. It was his last laugh.

(see ASSASSINATION, DEATH)

DREAM

Soon after his nomination for the presidency, Abraham Lincoln began having frightening dreams in which he saw himself dead. He told his wife and his most intimate friends about them. One of his friends, his former law partner Ward Lamon, who subsequently served as marshal of the District of Columbia during Lincoln's administration, wrote an account of these "death dreams" in his biography of Lincoln:

> How, it may be asked, could he make life tolerable, burdened as he was with that portentous horror, which, though visionary, and of trifling import in our eyes, was by his interpretation a premonition of impending doom? I answer in a word: His sense of duty to his country; his belief that "the inevitable" is right; and his innate and irrepressible humor.
>
> But the most startling incident in the life of Mr. Lincoln was a dream he had only a few days before his assassination. To him it was a thing of deadly import, and certainly no vision was ever fashioned more exactly like a dread reality. . . .
>
> After worrying over it for some days, Mr. Lincoln seemed no longer able to keep the secret. I give it as nearly in his own words as I can, from notes which I made immediately after its recital. There were only two or three persons present.
>
> The President was in a melancholy, meditative mood, and had been silent for some time. Mrs. Lincoln, who

was present, rallied him on his solemn visage and want of spirit. This seemed to arouse him, and, without seeming to notice her sally, he said, in slow and measured tones:

"It seems strange how much there is in the Bible about dreams. There are, I think, some sixteen chapters in the Old Testament and four or five in the New, in which dreams are mentioned; and there are many other passages scattered throughout the book which refer to visions. In the old days, God and His angels came to men in their sleep and made themselves known in dreams."

Mrs. Lincoln here remarked, "Why, you look dreadfully solemn; do you believe in dreams?"

"I can't say that I do," returned Mr. Lincoln, "but I had one the other night which has haunted me ever since. After it occurred the first time, I opened the Bible, and, strange as it may appear, it was the twenty-eighth chapter of Genesis, which relates the wonderful dream Jacob had. I turned to other passages, and seemed to encounter a dream or a vision wherever I looked. I kept on turning the leaves of the old book, and everywhere my eyes fell upon passages recording matters strangely in keeping with my own thoughts—supernatural visitations, dreams, visions, etc."

He now looked so serious and disturbed that Mrs. Lincoln exclaimed: "You frighten me! What is the matter?"

"I am afraid," said Mr. Lincoln, observing the effect his words had upon his wife, "that I have done wrong to mention the subject at all; but somehow the thing has got possession of me, and, like Banquo's ghost, it will not down."

This only inflamed Mrs. Lincoln's curiosity the more, and while bravely disclaiming any belief in dreams, she strongly urged him to tell the dream which seemed to have such a hold upon him, being seconded in this by another listener. Mr. Lincoln hesitated, but at length commenced very deliberately, his brow overcast with a shade of melancholy.

"About ten days ago," said he, "I retired very late. I

had been up waiting for important dispatches from the front. I could not have been long in bed when I fell into a slumber, for I was weary. I soon began to dream. There seemed to be a death-like stillness about me. Then I heard subdued sobs, as if a number of people were weeping.

"I thought I left my bed and wandered downstairs. There the silence was broken by the same pitiful sobbing, but the mourners were invisible. I went from room to room; no living person was in sight, but the same mournful sounds of distress met me as I passed along. It was light in all the rooms; every object was familiar to me; but where were all the people who were grieving as if their hearts would break? I was puzzled and alarmed. What could be the meaning of all this?

"Determined to find the cause of a state of things so mysterious and so shocking, I kept on until I arrived at the East Room, which I entered. There I met with a sickening surprise. Before me was a catafalque, on which rested a corpse wrapped in funeral vestments. Around it were stationed soldiers who were acting as guards; and there was a throng of people, some gazing mournfully upon the corpse, whose face was covered, others weeping pitifully.

" 'Who is dead in the White House?' I demanded of one of the soldiers.

" 'The President,' was his answer; 'he was killed by an assassin.'

"Then came a loud burst of grief from the crowd, which awoke me from my dream. I slept no more that night; and although it was only a dream, I have been strangely annoyed by it ever since."

"That is horrid!" said Mrs. Lincoln. "I wish you had not told it. I am glad I don't believe in dreams, or I should be in terror from this time forth."

"Well," responded Mr. Lincoln, thoughtfully, "it is only a dream, Mary."

(see DEATH, PHANTOM FUNERAL TRAIN)

DUTY

Let us have faith that right makes might, and in that faith let us to the end dare to do our duty as we understand it.

—Address at Cooper Union, New York,
February 27, 1860
(see MIGHT)

E

EDITORIALS

At the outset of the Civil War, military strategy was dictated by the large newspapers, whose editorial writers told the president and his generals precisely what had to be done.

Weary of all the well-meaning advice, President Lincoln cut short the presentation of yet another war plan by a New York newspaper correspondent:

"Your New York papers remind me of a little story. Some years ago, there was a gentleman traveling through Kansas on horseback. There were few settlements and no roads, and he lost his way. Then to make matters worse, as night came on, a terrific thunderstorm arose, and peal after peal of thunder, following flashes of lightning, shook the earth and momentarily illuminated the scene. The terrified traveler dismounted and led his horse, seeking to guide it as best he might by the flickering light of the quick flashes of lightning. All

of a sudden, a tremendous crash of thunder brought the
man to his knees in terror, and he cried out:

" 'O Lord! If it's all the same to you, give us a little
more light and a little less noise!' "

(see COUNSELORS, CRITICS)

EDUCATION

I desire to see the time when education—and by its
means, morality, sobriety, enterprise and industry—shall
become much more general than at present.

—Communication to the people of Sangamo County,
Illinois, March 9, 1832
[when Lincoln was a candidate for State Assembly]

Upon the subject of education . . . I can only say that I
view it as the most important subject which we as a
people may be engaged in.

—Communication, *Sangamo Journal*,
New Salem, Illinois, 1832

That everyone may receive at least a moderate education
. . . appears to be an object of vital importance.

—Communication, *Sangamo Journal*,
New Salem, Illinois, 1832

ELECTIONS

We cannot have free government without elections.

—"Response to a Serenade," November 10, 1864

If the rebellion should force us to forgo or postpone a
national election, it might fairly be said to have already
conquered and ruined us.

—"Response to a Serenade," November 10, 1864
(see VIOLENCE, VOTE)

EMANCIPATION PROCLAMATION

On September 21, 1862, President Lincoln called his cabinet to the White House for a special meeting.

Secretary of War Edwin M. Stanton recalled it later: "The President was reading a book and hardly noticed me as I came in. Finally he turned to us and said: 'Gentlemen, did you ever read anything of Artemus Ward?' " He held up a book by America's most famous humorist of the time. " 'Let me read a chapter that is very funny.' "

Lincoln proceeded to read aloud a sketch by Ward entitled "A High Handed Outrage at Utica." Stanton was so outraged at Lincoln's buffoonery that he almost got up and walked out. Lincoln read the entire piece and laughed heartily, but no one else joined in the merriment.

"Why don't you laugh?" Lincoln asked them. "With the fearful strain that is upon me night and day, if I did not laugh I should die, and you need this medicine as much as I do." The president then reached into his tall hat, which sat on the table, and pulled out a paper. "I have called you here upon very important business. I have prepared a little paper of much significance. I have said nothing to anyone, but I have made a promise to myself—and to my Maker. I am now going to fulfill that promise."

Lincoln then read in a firm voice the announcement of the Emancipation Proclamation:

On the first day of January in the year of our Lord, one thousand eight hundred and sixty-three, all persons held as slaves within any state, or designated part of a state, the people whereof shall then be in rebellion against the United States shall be then, thenceforward, and forever free.

The men of the cabinet were stunned. Stanton said later in praise: "If reading a chapter of Artemus Ward is a prelude to such a deed as this, the book should be filed among the archives of the nation and the author canonized!"

Abraham Lincoln considered the Emancipation Proclamation "the central act of my administration and the great event of the nineteenth century."

On January 1, when the Emancipation Proclamation was brought to President Lincoln by Secretary of State William H. Seward for signature, Lincoln picked up a pen, dipped it in ink, moved his hand to the place for signature, paused, and then withdrew his hand and dropped the pen.

After flexing his fingers for a few moments, Lincoln turned to Seward and explained: "I have been shaking hands since nine o'clock this morning, and my right arm is almost paralyzed. If my name ever goes into history, I know it will be for this act, and my whole soul is in it. If my hand trembles when I sign the Proclamation, all who examine the document hereafter will say: 'He hesitated.' "

He paused, breathed deeply, and took up the pen again.

Later Lincoln was told by Colonel McKaye of New York that there was widespread affection for him among the freed ex-slaves in the South. The president was deeply touched by this news. He told McKaye: "It is a momentous thing to be the instrument, under Providence, of the liberation of a race."

And by virtue of the power and for the purposes aforesaid, I do order and declare that all persons held as slaves within said designated states and parts of states are, and henceforward shall be, free; and that the executive Government of the United States, including the military and naval authorities thereof, will recognize and maintain the freedom of said persons.

—Emancipation Proclamation, January 1, 1863
(see SLAVERY)

EMBARRASSMENT

I have found that when one is embarrassed, usually the shortest way to get through with it is to quit talking or thinking about it, and go at something else.

—Speech, Cincinnati, Ohio, September 17, 1859

ENDS

Abraham Lincoln rarely confused the means and the ends. "One day when we were attending court at Bloomington, Illinois," recalled his friend and fellow lawyer Ward Lamon, "I was wrestling near the courthouse with someone who had challenged me. In the scuffle, I made a large rent in the rear of my trousers. Before I had time to change, I was called into court to take up a case. Since I had on a short coat, my misfortune was apparent, and one of the lawyers started a subscription paper, which was passed from one member of the bar to another, to buy me a pair of pants. Several put down ridiculous subscriptions, and finally the paper was laid in front of Lincoln. Glancing over it, he immediately wrote after his name, 'I can contribute nothing to the end in view.' "

(see PUNS)

ENEMIES

At an official reception during the Civil War, President Lincoln made a brief speech in which he referred to the Confederates as erring human beings, rather than as enemies to be destroyed.

An elderly lady, a fiery zealot for the Union cause, rebuked him for speaking kindly of the enemies of his country when he ought to be thinking of exterminating them.

"Why, Madam," replied Lincoln, "do I not destroy my enemies when I make them friends?"

(see CONFEDERATES, ESCAPE, FRIENDS)

ENTERPRISE

The prudent, penniless beginner in the world labors for wages awhile, saves a surplus with which to buy tools or land for himself; then labors on his own account another while, and at length hires another new beginner to help him. This is the just, and generous and prosperous system which opens the way to all—gives hope to all, and consequent energy, and progress, and improvement of condition to all.

—Annual Message to Congress, December 3, 1861
(see LABOR, PROPERTY, WORKERS)

EQUALITY

Four score and seven years ago, our fathers brought forth on this continent a new nation, conceived in liberty, and dedicated to the proposition that all men are created equal.

—Gettysburg Address, November 19, 1863

They [the signers of the Declaration of Independence] did not mean to assert the obvious untruth that all were then actually enjoying that equality, nor yet that they were about to confer it immediately upon them. In fact, they had no power to confer such a boon. They meant simply to declare the *right*; so that the *enforcement* of it might follow as fast as circumstances should permit.

—Speech, Springfield, Illinois, June 26, 1857

Our progress in degeneracy appears to me to be pretty rapid. As a nation we began by declaring that "all men are created equal." We now practically read it "all men are created equal, except Negroes." When the Know-Nothings get control, it will read "all men are created equal except Negroes and foreigners and Catholics." When it comes to this, I shall prefer emigrating to some country where they make no pretense of loving liberty—to Russia, for instance, where despotism can be taken pure, and without the base alloy of hypocrisy.

—Letter to Joshua F. Speed, August 24, 1855

Let us discard all this quibbling about this man and the other man—this race and that race and the other race as being inferior. . . . Let us discard all these things, and unite as one people throughout this land, until we shall once more stand up declaring that all men are created equal.

—Speech, Chicago, Illinois, July 10, 1858

I leave you, hoping that the lamp of liberty will burn in your bosoms, until there shall no longer be a doubt that all men are created free and equal.

—Speech, Chicago, Illinois, July 10, 1858
(see AMERICA, DECLARATION, LIBERTY)

ESCAPE

After General Robert E. Lee's surrender, President Lincoln was pressured by many in Washington to execute the Confederate leaders. General Benjamin F. Butler was one of those who demanded execution as the only fitting punishment for the treason of the rebel leaders who plunged the nation into Civil War.

While the fate of the Confederate leaders was still being deliberated, General Butler informed President Lincoln that the arch rebel, "Jake" Thompson, a Confederate commissioner, was attempting to slip through Maine in disguise, with the intention of disembarking from Portland and escaping to England.

"By permitting him to escape the penalties of treason, you sanction it," said General Butler.

President Lincoln was inclined to be merciful now that the war was over, and he did not want to alienate the South, now that it had been forcibly brought back into the Union. "Well," he said, "let me tell you a story. There was an Irish soldier here last summer, who had been induced by his friends time and again to join the temperance society, but had always broken away. He was finally given notice by his friends that if he violated his pledge once more, they would abandon him as an utterly hopeless vagrant. He made an earnest struggle to maintain his promise, but one night he was overcome by thirst and he stopped at a drug shop, where he espied a soda fountain. 'Mr. Doctor,' said he, 'give me, plase, a glass of soda-wather, an' if yez can put in a few drops of whiskey unbeknown to me, I'll be obleeged.'

"Now," continued Lincoln, "if 'Jake' Thompson is permitted to go through Maine unbeknown to anyone, what's the harm? So don't have him arrested. The fact

is, if these men could get away from the country unbeknown to us, it would save a world of trouble."

(see CONFEDERATES, ENEMIES, FRIENDS)

EVILS

To correct the evils, great and small, which spring from
want of sympathy and from positive enmity among
strangers, as nations or as individuals, is one of the highest functions of civilization.

—Speech, Milwaukee, Wisconsin, September 30, 1859

God did not place good and evil before man, telling him
to make his choice. On the contrary, he did tell him
there was one tree of the fruit of which he should not
eat, upon pain of certain death.

—Speech, Peoria, Illinois, October 16, 1854
(see GOD, RIGHT AND WRONG)

EXAGGERATION

During the Civil War Lincoln received a report from one
of his generals that, the president suspected, exagger-
ated the Union army's success. Claiming to have killed
hundreds of Confederates in battle, the general concluded by saying, "and our loss was twelve men killed,
wounded, and captured."

Lincoln said this statement reminded him of a man
who used to lecture about his travels abroad, but played
fast and loose with facts and figures. A friend who traveled with him repeatedly cautioned him to keep his facts
and figures proportionate to the truth and to each other.

Realizing that he was prone to exaggerate on occasion, the lecturer asked his friend, who always sat behind him on the platform, to yank his coattails whenever
he drifted into hyperbole. The friend agreed.

In his next lecture, the orator told the audience about a tall building he had seen in Europe. "And that building," he said with a little too much enthusiasm, "was a mile and a half long, and really it must have been a mile high!"

At that moment he felt his friend pull his coattails. He was trying to think how to salvage his credibility and make amends for his exaggeration when someone from the audience called out: "And how *wide* was the building?"

The lecturer replied quickly, "Oh, *just about a foot.*"

(see CONFEDERATES)

EXPERIMENT

Many experiments were tried out of the necessity to arm, equip, and feed the army economically. President Lincoln was the first to take an interest in any experimental new weapon that might tip the balance of the war, but he cautioned his generals against experimenting with the lives of the soldiers.

"One of these generals, who has a scheme for 'condensing' rations, is willing to swear his life away that his idea, when carried to perfection, will reduce the cost of feeding the Union troops to almost nothing," said Lincoln, skeptically.

"It reminds me of the story of an Irishman—a cabman—who had a notion that he could induce his horse to live entirely on shavings. The latter he could get for nothing, while corn and oats were pretty high-priced. So he daily lessened the amount of food to the horse, substituting shavings for the corn and oats abstracted, so that the horse wouldn't know his rations were being cut down.

"However, just as he had achieved success in his experiment, and the horse had been taught to live without any other food than shavings, the ungrateful animal up and died—and he had to buy another.

"So far as this general is concerned, I'm afraid the soldiers will all be dead by the time his experiment is demonstrated as thoroughly successful."

(see GENERALS)

EXPLANATIONS

I fear explanations explanatory of things explained.

—Referring to Stephen A. Douglas
in the Lincoln-Douglas debates
(see ARGUMENT, DEBATE)

EYES

As President, I have no eyes but constitutional eyes; I cannot see you.

—To the Confederate commissioners
from South Carolina, 1861
(see SECESSION)

F

FAILURE

The probability that we may fail in the struggle ought not to deter us from the support of a cause we believe to be just.

—Speech, Springfield, Illinois, December 1839

I find quite as much material for a lecture in those points wherein I have failed, as in those wherein I have been moderately successful.

—Notes for a law lecture, July 1, 1850

Let us, therefore, study the incidents of this as philosophy to learn wisdom from, and none of them as wrongs to be revenged.

—"Response to a Serenade," November 10, 1864
(see DEFEAT)

FAVORITISM

A well-bred woman with a haughty air accosted President Lincoln at a reception and made this appeal:

"Mr. President, you must give me a colonel's commission for my son. Sir, I demand it, not as a favor, but as a right. Sir, my grandfather fought at Lexington. My uncle was the only man who did not run away at Bladensburg. My father fought at New Orleans, sir, and my husband was killed at Monterrey."

Lincoln's bushy eyebrows rose a notch up his furrowed forehead. "Madam," he said, "your family has done enough for the country. It is time to give somebody else a chance."

(see ANCESTRY)

FEET

Six feet four inches tall, Abraham Lincoln towered over most men. But one day while inspecting a Union army regiment, he encountered a soldier nearly seven feet in height.

"Hello, comrade," said President Lincoln, gazing earnestly upwards at the giant. "Say, how do you know when your feet are cold?"

(see COLDS, LEGS)

FLATTERY

When my friend, Judge Douglas, came to Chicago . . . he complimented me as being a "kind, amiable and intelligent gentleman." . . . I was not very much accustomed to flattery, and it came the sweeter to me. I was rather like the Hoosier with gingerbread, when he said

78

he reckoned he loved it better than any other man, and
got less of it.

—Speech, at Ottawa, Illinois, July 31, 1858
(see PUNISHMENT)

FLOWERS

"Goodbye, Mr. Lincoln," said a grateful lady whose
husband Lincoln had released from the army to support
the family. "I shall probably never see you again till we
meet in heaven." She burst into tears.

Lincoln kindly took her hand and led her to the door
of his White House office. "I am afraid with all my troubles I shall never get to the resting place you speak of,"
he replied. "But if I do, I am sure I shall find you. That
you wish me to get there is, I believe, the best wish you
could make for me. Goodbye."

After her departure he turned to his friend Joshua
Speed, who was in the room with him and remarked:
"It is more than many can often say, that in doing right
one has made two people happy in one day."

Lincoln sighed, then added: "Speed, die when I may,
I want it said of me by those who know me best that I
have always plucked a thistle and planted a flower when
I thought a flower would grow."

(see GOOD, RELIGION)

FOOL

It is true that you may fool all the people some of the
time; you can even fool some of the people all the time;
but you can't fool all of the people all the time.

—McClure, *Lincoln's Yarns and Stories*, 1904
(see ADVICE)

FORGIVENESS

Asked why he was willing to forgive an old nemesis, Lincoln replied, "I choose always to make my statute of limitations a short one."

(see ENEMIES, REPRIEVE)

I am a patient man—always willing to forgive on the Christian terms of repentance, and also to give ample *time* for repentance.

—Letter to Reverdy Johnson, July 26, 1862

FREEDOM

I have always thought that all men should be free.

—Address to an Indiana Regiment, March 17, 1865

In giving freedom to the slave we assure freedom to the free—honorable alike in what we give and what we preserve.

—Message to Congress, December 1, 1862

Those who deny freedom to others deserve it not for themselves.

—Attributed
(see LIBERTY, SLAVERY)

FREEDOM OF SPEECH

Several prominent members of Lincoln's party opposed his reelection in 1864. Senator Benjamin Wade of Ohio, Henry Winter Davis of Maryland, and Wendell Phillips all made eloquent speeches against Lincoln and his policy.

Asked if he was concerned by the opposition expressed by these distinguished men, Lincoln shook his head and said: "I shall not complain of them. I accord them the utmost freedom of speech and liberty of the press, but shall not change the policy I have adopted in the full belief that I am right.

"I feel on this subject as an old Illinois farmer once expressed himself while eating cheese. He was interrupted in the midst of his repast by the entrance of his son, who exclaimed, 'Hold on, dad! There's bugs in that there cheese you're eating!'

" 'Never mind, son,' said he, as he kept on munching his cheese, 'if they can stand it I can.' "

(see QUALIFICATIONS, SKUNKS)

FRIENDS

"What is your definition of a friend?" a visitor to the White House once asked President Lincoln.

Lincoln stroked his beard reflectively before he answered, "One who has the same enemies you have."

The loss of enemies does not compensate for the loss of friends.

—Letter to William H. Seward, June 30, 1862
(see ENEMIES)

FUNERAL

The humorist Petroleum Nasby recalled that during his interview with President Lincoln the name was raised of a recently deceased Illinois politician, the magnitude of whose achievements was far exceeded by the magnitude of his ego.

"His funeral, quite surprisingly, was attended by nearly a thousand people," remarked Nasby.

"That many? If he had known how big a funeral he

would have had," said Lincoln, "I think he would have died years ago."

FUTURE

The best thing about the future is that it comes only one day at a time.

—Attributed

GENERALS

P. T. Barnum brought his circus to Washington during the Civil War. Huge crowds came to see the world-famous midgets, General Tom Thumb and Admiral Nutt. Lincoln came, too, and paid his respects. "You have some pretty small generals," he told Barnum, "but I think I can beat you."

President Lincoln tried out a succession of generals, replacing each one in turn before he finally found, late in 1862 in the person of Ulysses S. Grant, what he was looking for: a general who could win the war.

There was no shortage of aspiring generals. "The fact is, I have got more pegs than I have holes to put them in," Lincoln explained to one who was denied command. But there was a shortage of aggressive generals who were capable of winning decisive military victories. Lincoln could not countenance failure and replaced not only those commanders who suffered defeats but those who failed to win victories.

Lincoln quickly lost confidence in generals who repeatedly called for reinforcements. Hearing that one general had requested more men, Lincoln refused. "He's killed off enough men already," said the president. "I don't mean Confederates—our own men. What's the use in sending volunteers down to him if they're only used to fill graves?"

General George B. McClellan infuriated Lincoln when, after General Robert E. Lee had been beaten at Malvern Hill in seven days of fighting, with Richmond only twelve miles away, McClellan retired to Harrison's Landing instead of driving onward to the Confederate capital. Lincoln resolved to relieve McClellan of command and find a more aggressive general.

After General Ambrose E. Burnside's defeat at Fredericksburg, he was replaced by General Joseph Hooker. Hooker, however, failed to capitalize on another opportunity to hurt Lee. "If the head of Lee's army is at Martinsburg, and the tail of it on the flank road between Fredericksburg and Chancellorsville, the animal must be very slim somewhere," Lincoln wrote to Hooker. "Could you not break him?"

After Hooker's disaster at Chancellorsville, he was relieved by General George G. Meade, who won at Gettysburg, but failed to follow through and pursue Lee's army in retreat; General William S. Rosencrans was humiliated at Chickamauga and yielded his place to Ulysses S. Grant, who, alone among Lincoln's generals, never suffered a defeat.

Lincoln was not at all intimidated by generals and frequently expressed annoyance with them and their egotism. Once he denied a request for a command with this explanation:

"Suppose you had a large cattleyard full of all sorts of cattle—cows, oxen, bulls—and you kept killing and selling and disposing of your cows and oxen, in one way and another—taking good care of your bulls. By and by you would find that you had nothing but a yard full of old bulls, good for nothing under heaven. Now, it will be just so with the army, if I don't stop making brigadier generals."

(see AID, ASSISTANCE, DIVORCE, GRANT, HEROISM, HOOKER, MCCLELLAN, RESIGNATION)

GENEROSITY

Abraham Lincoln was a kind-hearted man who found it difficult to turn down the many requests made of a man in his position.

"I thank God I was not born a woman," Lincoln once remarked, "because I never could refuse a request that was not apparently dishonest."

GENIUS

Towering genius disdains a beaten path. It seeks regions hitherto unexplored.

—Address to the Young Men's Lyceum, January 27, 1838

GETTYSBURG ADDRESS

The Gettysburg Address is regarded as one of the greatest examples of oratory in the the history of the world, yet the entire speech contains fewer than three hundred words and required only two minutes to deliver. According to the poet Louis Untermeyer, "Abraham Lincoln wrote the Gettysburg Address while travelling from Washington to Gettysburg on the back of an envelope." But this is a myth. There are two extant drafts of the speech, one of them composed on Executive Mansion stationery, probably before Lincoln's departure from

Washington. He continued revising and polishing the speech up to the last minute.

The featured speaker at the dedication of the Gettysburg cemetery was Edward Everett, a former governor of Massachusetts known for his oratory. He spoke for one hour and fifty-eight minutes.

Then President Lincoln stood up and spoke for two minutes. When he sat down he felt disappointed. He shook his head. "That speech won't scour," he said to his friend Ward Lamon. "It's a flat failure."

Many critics concurred. "The ceremony was rendered ludicrous by the sallies of that poor President Lincoln," wrote the *Times* correspondent, who dismissed the speech as "dull and commonplace."

Edward Everett disagreed. "I should be glad," he wrote to the president, "if I could flatter myself that I came as near to the central idea of the occasion in two hours as you did in two minutes."

(see HURRY, BIOGRAPHY 1863)

GOD

At a White House dinner, a churchman offered a benediction and closed with the pious affirmation: "The Lord is on our side."

When President Lincoln did not respond to this sentiment, someone asked him, "Don't you believe, Mr. President, that the Lord is always on the side of the right?"

"I am not concerned about that," was Lincoln's answer, "for we know that the Lord is always on the side of the right. My concern is that I and this nation should be on the Lord's side."

Men are not flattered by being shown that there has been a difference of purpose between the Almighty and them.

—Letter to Thurlow Weed, March 15, 1865

The Almighty has His own purposes.

—Second Inaugural Address, 1865
(see EVILS, PRAYER, SALVATION)

GOOD

The following lines were found written in young Abraham Lincoln's hand, at the bottom of a page on which he had been ciphering as a schoolboy:

Abraham Lincoln
his hand and pen
he will be good
but god Knows When

At that age Lincoln did not write "God" with an upper case "G."

(see FLOWERS)

GOVERNMENT

If all men were just, there still would be *some*, though not *so much*, need of government.

—Fragment on government, July 1, 1854

The legitimate object of government is to do for the people what needs to be done, but which they cannot, by individual effort, do at all, or do so well, for themselves.

—Fragment on government, July 1, 1854

No man is good enough to govern another man without that other's consent.

—Speech, Peoria, Illinois, October 16, 1854

It is safe to assert that no government proper ever had a provision in its organic law for its own termination.

—First Inaugural Address, March 4, 1861

It has long been a grave question whether any government, not too strong for the liberties of its people, can be strong enough to maintain its existence in great emergencies.

—"Response to a Serenade," November 10, 1864
(see BIG GOVERNMENT, MAJORITY RULE,
REPUBLICANISM, RIGHTS)

GRANT, ULYSSES S.

President Lincoln came to regard Ulysses S. Grant more highly than any of his other generals and ultimately put him in command of all the Union armies. Observing that Grant never gave up an inch of the ground he had gained in battle, Lincoln remarked to General Benjamin F. Butler, "When General Grant once gets possessed of a place he seems to hang on to it as if he inherited it."

Grant had his detractors, though, some of whom were motivated by jealousy. One influential politician warned Lincoln not to trust Grant: "General Grant is a drunkard. He is not himself half the time and cannot be relied upon."

"So Grant is a drunk, is he?" mused Lincoln.

"Yes, he is, and I can prove it," was the answer.

"Well, all I want to know is the brand of whiskey General Grant uses," said Lincoln.

"The brand of whiskey?"

"Yes," replied the president. "I would like to furnish the same brand to my other generals."

When Lincoln was nominated for a second term in 1864, some supporters told him the only way he could be defeated would be if General Grant took Richmond and then decided to run for president against him.

"Well," said Lincoln, folding his arms, "I feel very much like the man who, after a serious talk with his doctor, said he didn't want to die particularly, but if he had to die that was precisely the disease he would like to die of."

(see ASSISTANCE, GENERALS)

HANDSOME

Republican Congressman Thaddeus Stevens of Pennsylvania was one of the many leaders who criticized President Lincoln for granting too many pardons during the Civil War, but one day Stevens brought a woman from his home state to plead for her son, who was condemned for sleeping at his post.

"Now, Thad, what would you do in this case, if you happened to be president?" Lincoln asked Stevens.

Stevens sheepishly replied that in this particular case he would certainly pardon the boy because of extenuating circumstances.

Lincoln scribbled something on a piece of paper and handed it to the woman. "Here, madam," he said, "is your son's pardon."

She wept with gratitude. As Stevens escorted her from the White House, she turned to him and said, "I knew it was a lie."

"What do you mean?" asked Stevens.

"When I left home yesterday," she answered, "my neighbors told me that I would find Mr. Lincoln an ugly man. It was a lie; he is the handsomest man I ever saw in my life!"

(see HOMELINESS, PARDON)

HAPPINESS

Most folks are about as happy as they make up their minds to be.

—Attributed

HAT

At his first inauguration on March 4, 1861, President Lincoln was sworn in on the eastern portico of the Capitol. He arrived on the platform carrying the manuscript of his First Inaugural Address, a cane, and his best tall silk hat. He set the cane down under the table, but he did not know what to do with the hat.

His old rival Senator Stephen A. Douglas came to the rescue. Douglas stepped up, took the hat, and returned to his seat. "If I can't be president," said Douglas, "I can at least hold his hat."

(see BARTENDER, DEBATE, DOUGLAS, BIOGRAPHY 1842)

HAWAII

One of the most eagerly sought-after appointments in the government was the commissionership of Hawaii, then called the Sandwich Islands.

President Lincoln listened politely to a delegation that appeared before him to beg the commission for a certain gentleman who, they said, in addition to being eminently qualified for the post, was in poor health and would benefit from the Hawaiian climate.

"Gentleman," said Lincoln, "I am sorry to say that there are eight other applicants for the place, and they are all sicker than your man."

(see APPLICANTS, FAVORITISM, JACKASS, OFFICE SEEKERS)

HEROISM

He who does something at the head of one regiment will eclipse him who does nothing at the head of a hundred.

—Letter to General David Hunter, 1862
(see GENERALS)

HITCHHIKING

Abe Lincoln did some hitchhiking in his younger days. Of course, in those days the best a hitchhiker could hope for would be a ride in a horse-drawn carriage.

One hot summer afternoon Lincoln was walking down a dusty road when a stranger came along driving a buggy. Lincoln, whose coat was slung over his shoulder, called out to the driver: "Sir, will you be so kind as to take my overcoat to town for me?"

The man in the buggy was perplexed by this request but agreed to it. "But how will you get your overcoat back again?" he asked.

"Oh, that's easy," said Lincoln, putting on his coat. "I'll stay right inside it."

HOG

When approached by a sightseer who requested a permit to pass behind the lines and visit the field of Bull

Run, President Lincoln denied it with this explanation: "Let me tell you a story about a hog. A man in Cortland County raised a porker of such unusual size that strangers went out of their way to see it. One day a curious stranger met the old gentleman and inquired about the huge hog.

" 'Wall, yes,' said the old geezer, 'I've got such a critter, mi'ty big un; but I guess I'll have to charge you about a dollar for lookin' at him.'

"The stranger looked at the old man for a minute or so, pulled out a dollar, handed it to him and started to leave. 'Hold on!' said the old fellow. 'Don't you want to see the hog?'

" 'No,' said the stranger. 'I have seen as big a hog as I want to see.' "

Lincoln cleared his throat. "And you will find that the case with yourself, if you should happen to see a few live rebels there as well as dead ones."

(see CORPSES)

HOLMES, OLIVER WENDELL

When President Lincoln paid a visit to the front, during the Confederate attack on Fort Stevens, near Washington, D.C., it was young Oliver Wendell Holmes who showed him around. Holmes, a general's aide, pointed out the enemy in the distance.

Lincoln, tall hat and all, stood up to get a better look, and immediately drew musket fire from the Confederate trenches.

"Get down, you fool!" cried Holmes, grabbing the president by the arm and pulling him down under cover. Once safe, Holmes suddenly realized what he had said. He waited in dread of disciplinary action.

Lincoln kept him waiting until, just before departing,

he said to Holmes with a wink, "Goodbye, Captain Holmes. I'm glad you know how to talk to a civilian."

(see HUSTLE)

HOMELINESS

Abraham Lincoln made many self-deprecating jokes about his homely appearance. Once while speaking to a convention of newspaper editors in Bloomington, Indiana, he said he felt out of place there because of his lack of editorial credentials and he wondered whether he should have come at all. "I feel like I once did when I met a woman riding on horseback in the woods. As I stopped to let her pass, she also stopped and looked at me intently and said, 'I do believe you are the ugliest man I ever saw.'

" 'Madam,' I said, 'you are probably right, but I can't help it.'

" 'No,' said she, 'you can't help it, but you might stay at home.' "

(see HANDSOME, PHOTOGRAPH, PORTRAIT)

HONEST ABE

Abraham Lincoln's honesty was not universally appreciated. In fact, even in his home state there were many who considered him dishonest. According to the *Illinois State Register* newspaper, he was "the craftiest and most dishonest politician that ever disgraced an office in America." Even his hometown newspaper reviled him: "How the greatest butchers of antiquity sink into insignificance when their crimes are contrasted with those of Abraham Lincoln."

Nevertheless, Lincoln is the only president besides George Washington whose honesty has become legendary. It was during his shopkeeping days in New Salem that young Lincoln earned the reputation for integrity that led to the sobriquet "Honest Abe." The nickname stuck with him through succeeding years and careers. The following incident illustrates why.

Soon after his store went out of business, Abraham Lincoln received his first political appointment. At the age of twenty-four he was named postmaster of New Salem—a sinecure for which he was paid an annual salary of $55.70.

In 1836 the New Salem post office was closed, but in those days bureaucracy was even slower than today, and it was several years before an agent arrived from Washington to settle accounts with ex-postmaster Lincoln.

By that time Lincoln had started a fledgling law practice and was struggling to make ends meet. When the agent located him at his law office and informed him that seventeen dollars was due the government, Lincoln crossed the room, pulled out an old trunk, opened it up, and removed a yellowed cotton rag bound with string. He untied it, spread out the cloth, and there was seventeen dollars.

The agent expressed surprise to see that the money had been untouched after all these years, even though Lincoln was living in poverty.

Lincoln explained, "I never use any man's money but my own."

(see ALGER)

HONESTY

No men living are more worthy to be trusted than those who toil up from poverty, none less inclined to take or touch aught which they have not honestly earned. Let

95

them beware of surrendering a political power which they already possess.

—Annual Message to Congress, December 3, 1861

HOOKER, JOSEPH

When President Lincoln could no longer tolerate General George B. McClellan's "waiting campaign" tactics, he relieved McClellan and placed General Joseph Hooker in charge of the army.

General Hooker, eager to convey the impression of vigorous activity, reported his movements to the president in a dispatch labeled "Headquarters in the Saddle."

"The trouble with Hooker," remarked Lincoln, examining the dispatch, "is that he's got his headquarters where his hindquarters ought to be."

(see GENERALS)

HOPE

There was a lull in the fighting of the Civil War when President Lincoln received a telegram from Cumberland Gap informing him that gunfire had been heard near Knoxville, where General Ambrose E. Burnside was reported to be in much peril.

"I am glad to hear this news," said the president calmly.

When his aides expressed surprise at his remark, Lincoln explained:

"You see, it reminds me of Mistress Sallie Ward, a neighbor of mine, who had a very large family. Occasionally one of her numerous prodigy would be heard crying in some out-of-the-way place, whereupon Mrs.

Ward would heave a sigh and say, 'There's one of my children, not dead yet.' "

(see GENERALS)

HORSE

When Abraham Lincoln was a young lawyer in Illinois, he was once called out of town on a critical case. He hired a horse from a livery stable for transportation. Returning a few days later, he installed the horse in its stall and casually asked the owner, "Tell me, do you keep this horse for funerals?"

"Certainly not!" snapped the owner indignantly.

"That's good," replied Lincoln wryly, "because if you did the corpse wouldn't get there in time for the resurrection."

(see LAZINESS)

HORSE TRADE

One time, during his days on the legal circuit, Abraham Lincoln and a judge began to banter about horse trading; finally, they agreed that they would make a trade the next morning at nine o'clock. Neither man was to see the other man's horse before that hour, and if either man backed out he was to forfeit thirty-five dollars.

The next morning at nine o'clock, the judge sauntered up, leading the sorriest-looking specimen of a horse ever seen in that part of the state—a skinny, bony, flea-bitten creature not much bigger than a dog. Shortly afterward, Lincoln arrived with a wooden sawhorse upon his shoulders.

The judge looked at Lincoln's sawhorse and Lincoln looked at the judge's puny horse. "Well, Judge," said

Lincoln, "this is the first time I ever got the worst of it in a horse trade."

(see PUNS)

HUMAN NATURE

Human nature will not change. In any future great national trial, compared with men of this, we shall have as weak and as strong, as silly and as wise, as bad and as good.

—"Response to a Serenade," November 10, 1864

Human action can be modified to some extent, but human nature cannot be changed.

—Attributed

HUMOR

Abraham Lincoln was probably the only American president who could be called a humorist. Other presidents have been known for their wit, but only Lincoln could truly be called an artist of the comic.

"It was as a humorist that he towered above all other men it was ever my lot to meet," said H. C. Whitney, a lawyer who traveled the circuit with Lincoln in Illinois.

Lincoln called laughter "the joyous, beautiful, universal evergreen of life." It was also the best antidote to despair. Abraham Lincoln suffered from bouts of melancholy, which grew more severe in later years, and his sense of humor was perhaps his best defense against the depression to which this sensitive soul was susceptible. "I laugh because if I didn't I would weep," he explained. A prominent New York editor, Henry J. Raymond, offered this insight: "It has been well said by a profound critic of Shakespeare, and it occurs to me as very appropriate in this connection, that 'the spirit which held the woe of Lear and the tragedy of "Hamlet" would have broken had it not also had the humor of the "Merry Wives of Windsor" and the merriment of the "Midsummer Night's Dream." ' This is as true of Mr. Lincoln as it was of Shakespeare. The capacity to tell and enjoy a good anecdote no doubt prolonged his life."

For Lincoln, humor was much more than a mere psychological defense mechanism. It was a way of finding the shortest common denominator to reach the hearts and minds of his countrymen.

It is doubtful if any American president has used humor more frequently or more effectively than did Lincoln. Lincoln was the storytelling president who used jokes and anecdotes to illustrate his points, to humanize his principles, and to keep spirits up in a time of national tragedy. Carl Sandburg, author of a monumental six-volume biography, *Abraham Lincoln*, wrote: "People looked at Lincoln, searching his face, thinking about his words and ways, ready to believe he was a Great Man. Then he would spill over with a joke or tell of some new horse-play of wit or humor in the next county. The barriers tumbled. He was again a strange friend, a neighbor, a friendly stranger, no far-off Great Man at all."

Lincoln was the political pinnacle of an American heritage of the sympathetic, homespun, horse-sense humorist who, though untutored, wielded a rough-cut, diamond-edged wit and wisdom: a lineage that began with Benjamin Franklin and included Mark Twain; Josh Billings; and later, Will Rogers.

Lincoln loved the western humor of his time and prized it as something quintessentially American. "Next to William Shakespeare," he said, "Josh Billings is the greatest judge of human nature the world has ever seen."

Some scholars contend that it was Lincoln who made

western humor respectable, carrying out on the political stage what Mark Twain later accomplished on the literary stage. According to Fred Lewis Pattee, "this man of the West . . . stood in the limelight of the Presidency, transacting the nation's business with anecdotes from the frontier circuits, meeting hostile critics with shrewd border philosophy. . . ."

Lincoln's humorous stories always had a point. He learned early in life that a good story would not only bolster an argument but break down resistance and build up goodwill with all kinds of people. "He knew that the apt saying or anecdote, expressive of a principle or truth, constituted one of his greatest assets," wrote folklorist B. A. Botkin in *A Treasury of American Folklore.* "From the prize story-teller of his community and its spokesman at all the neighborhood gatherings, he rose to be story-teller to the nation and the voice of the people. He is our only folk hero who is also a folk artist. Akin to Aesop and Poor Richard, he differs from our other great folk story-teller, Mark Twain, in that he was not a professional humorist." Yet, unlike Twain, he was a professional statesman.

Lincoln spoke with a folk wisdom that was proverbial. The storytelling president was not merely the people's choice—he was the people's voice. Ultimately, Lincoln rose to the stature of a joke-telling American prophet, one who, as Botkin put it, "raised the wisecrack to the level of scripture."

(see JOKING, PUNS, STORYTELLING, WEDDING)

HURRY

President Lincoln was late for the train to Gettysburg on the day he was to deliver his immortal speech. When his aides expressed fears that he would miss the train, he calmed them with a little story. "You fellows remind me of the day they were going to hang the horse thief. The road to the hanging place was so crowded with people on their way to the execution that the wagon carrying the prisoner was delayed. As more and more people pushed their way ahead of the wagon, the prisoner called out, 'What's your hurry? There ain't going to be any fun till I get there!' "

(see GETTYSBURG)

HUSBANDS

"Well," said Abraham Lincoln after a painful compromise, "I feel about that a good deal like a man named Hennessy I once knew felt about his wife. He was one of your meek men, and had the reputation, not undeserved, of being badly henpecked. One day his wife was seen switching him out of the house. A little later a neighbor met him on the street and said:

" 'Hennessy, I have always stood up for you, as you know, but I am not going to any longer. Any man who will stand quietly and take a switching from his wife deserves to be horsewhipped.'

"Hennessy looked up with a wink and patted his friend on the back.

" 'Now don't get riled,' said he. 'Why, it didn't hurt me any, and you've no idea what a power of good it did Sarah Ann!' "

HUSTLE

As President Lincoln was stopping by the War Office once, he collided with an officer who was in a great hurry.

The officer slam-banged into the president and then,

recognizing the tall figure, apologized profusely. "Ten thousand pardons!" he exclaimed.

"One is enough," said Lincoln with a grin. "I wish the whole army would charge like that!"

(see HOLMES)

I

IMMORTALITY

Surely God would not have created such a being as man
. . . to exist only for a day! No, no, man was made for
immortality.

—Attributed

INTEGRITY

I am not bound to win, but I am bound to be true. I am
not bound to succeed, but I am bound to live up to what
light I have.

—Attributed
(see CONSCIENCE)

INVENTOR

It is a little-known fact that Abraham Lincoln was a pat-
ented inventor. On May 22, 1849, Lincoln received approval of his patent for a device to float vessels over

shoals by inflating cylinders. The shipping industry did not embrace this new technological development with great fervor, but the invention illustrates Lincoln's practical ingenuity.

J

JACKASS

On one occasion when President Lincoln was beleaguered by job seekers, he told this story:

An eccentric old king was so much bothered by bad weather that he hired a prophet to prophesy the royal weather for him. One day, as the king was dressing for an important engagement, he asked the weather prophet what the weather would be like.

"It will be a bright, clear night," predicted the prophet.

The king, following the advice of his prophet, put on a light suit and left his umbrella in the palace closet as he started off. On the road he chanced to meet an old farmer riding a jackass, holding an umbrella over his head.

"Why do you have an umbrella, old-timer?" asked the king. "There's not a cloud in the sky."

"It's going to rain," said the farmer.

Sure enough, a little while later the sky swelled full of big black clouds and it began to pour. The king was soaked to the skin, and his fine suit was ruined.

The next day, the king sent for the farmer. "I want to hire you as my weather prophet," he said.

"Sire, it ain't me," said the farmer. "It's my jackass. Every time that critter's ears hang down low, it's sure to rain."

"Very well," said the king. "Go home, old man. I'll hire the jackass."

And so he did. And this is why there are so many jackasses in Washington. Now ever since that time, every jackass wants an office.

(see APPLICANTS, FAVORITISM, HAWAII, OFFICE SEEKERS)

JACKSON, ANDREW

Abraham Lincoln accused the Democrats of riding the military coattails of Andrew Jackson long after Jackson's retirement from the White House. In a speech in the House of Representatives on July 27, 1848, Lincoln put it this way:

"A fellow once advertised that he had made a discovery by which he could make a new man out of an old one and have enough of the stuff left to make a little yellow dog. Just such a discovery has General Jackson's popularity been to you. You not only twice made president of him out of it, but you have had enough of the stuff left to make presidents of several comparatively small men since, and it is your chief reliance now to make still another."

JEFFERSON, THOMAS

All honor to Jefferson—to the man who, in the concrete pressure of a struggle for national independence by a single people, had the coolness, forecast and sagacity to introduce into a merely revolutionary document an abstract truth, applicable to all men and all times, and so to embalm it there, that today, and in all coming days, it shall be a rebuke and a stumbling block to the very harbingers of reappearing tyranny and oppression.

—Letter to Henry Pierce and others, April 6, 1859
(see DECLARATION)

JOKING

Abraham Lincoln was not only a teller of many jokes, he was a subject of many jokes as well. He declared that his favorite among the many "Lincoln jokes" printed in the newspapers was the following:

"Two Quakeresses were riding on the railroad and were heard discussing the probable outcome of the war.

" 'I think,' said the first, 'that Jefferson Davis will succeed.'

" 'Why does thee think so?' asked the other.

" 'Because he is a praying man.'

" 'And so is Abraham a praying man,' the other objected.

" 'Yes,' replied the first, 'but the Lord will think Abraham is joking.' "

(see HUMOR)

JUDGE

Of a certain judge who had a harsh reputation as a "hanging judge," Abraham Lincoln remarked: "He held the strongest ideas of rigid government and close construction that I ever met. He would hang a man for blowing his nose on the street, but he would quash the indictment if it failed to specify which hand he blew it with!"

JUDICIAL POWER

If the policy of the government upon vital questions affecting the whole people is to be irrevocably fixed by decisions of the Supreme Court . . . the people will have ceased to be their own rulers, having to that extent practically resigned their government into the hands of that eminent tribunal.

—First Inaugural Address, March 4, 1861

JURORS

During jury selection, an opposing lawyer objected to a certain juror on the ground that the man knew Mr. Lincoln, and since this objection was a reflection upon the honor of a lawyer, Judge Davis overruled the objection.

Abraham Lincoln then tried the same tactic, examining some prospective jurors and finding out that they knew his opponent. The judge scolded Lincoln for this tactic. "Now, Mr. Lincoln, you are wasting time. The mere fact that a juror knows your opponent does not disqualify him."

"No, Your Honor," Lincoln answered drily, "but I am afraid some of the gentlemen may *not* know him, which would place me at a disadvantage."

(see DISCREDIT)

K

KENNEDY ASSASSINATION PARALLELS

The parallels between the assassinations of Abraham Lincoln and John F. Kennedy have intrigued many history buffs. These are the parallels that have been noted:

* Lincoln was elected president in 1860. Kennedy was elected president in 1960.

* Lincoln's first important public office was in the House of Representatives, to which he was elected in 1847. Kennedy's first important public office was in the House of Representatives, to which he was elected in 1947.

* Lincoln tried unsuccessfully to win his party's vice-presidential nomination in 1856. Kennedy tried unsuccessfully to win his party's vice-presidential nomination in 1956.

* Lincoln lost a son while in the White House—Willie died of a respiratory condition at age eleven. Kennedy lost a son while in the White House—Patrick died of a

respiratory condition just thirty-nine hours after his birth.

* Lincoln had an aide named John Kennedy who advised him not to go to Ford's Theater the night he was shot. Kennedy had an aide named Lincoln (Evelyn) who advised him not to go to Dallas, where he was shot.

* Lincoln was shot in the back of the head on a Friday—in fact, it was Good Friday—while he was sitting next to his wife. Kennedy was shot in the back of the head on a Friday while he was sitting next to his wife.

* Lincoln's assassin, John Wilkes Booth, whose full name has fifteen letters in it, was a southerner who shot the president in a theater and was himself shot dead before he could be brought to trial. Kennedy's alleged assassin, Lee Harvey Oswald, whose full name has fifteen letters in it, was a southerner who was arrested in a theater, and was shot dead before he could be brought to trial.

* Lincoln was succeeded in the White House by his vice-president, a southerner named Johnson—Andrew Johnson—who was born in 1808. Kennedy was succeeded in the White House by his vice-president, a southerner named Johnson—Lyndon B. Johnson—who was born in 1908.

One final ironic fact is that the car in which Kennedy was riding when he was assassinated was a Lincoln Continental limousine.

(see ASSASSINATION, BOOTH, DEATH)

LABOR

There is no permanent class of hired laborers among us. Twenty-five years ago I was a hired laborer. The hired laborer of yesterday labors on his own account today, and will hire others to labor for him tomorrow.

—Fragment on free labor, September 17, 1859

Labor is prior to, and independent of, capital. Capital is only the fruit of labor, and could never have existed if labor had not first existed. Labor is the superior of capital, and deserves much the higher consideration. Capital has its rights, which are as worthy of protection as any other rights.

—First Annual Message to Congress, December 3, 1861

And, inasmuch as most good things are produced by labor, it follows that such things of right belong to those whose labor has produced them. But it has so happened in all ages of the world, that *some* have labored and *oth-*

ers have, without labor, enjoyed a large proportion of the fruits. This is wrong, and should not continue. To secure to each laborer the whole product of his labor, or as nearly as possible, is a most worthy object of any good government.

—Fragment of a tariff discussion, December 1, 1847

I hold that if the Almighty had ever made a set of men that should do all the eating and none of the work, He would have made them with mouths only and no hands; and if He had ever made another class that He intended should do all the work and no eating, He would have made them with hands and no mouths.

—"Mud-sill Theory of Labor"
Address to Wisconsin State Agricultural Society
September 30, 1859
(see CAPITAL, CAPITALIST, ENTERPRISE, PROPERTY, WORKERS)

LATIN

As a trial attorney in Illinois, Abraham Lincoln argued many cases before juries, and it was his habit never to use a word that the dullest juror could not comprehend. For this reason he avoided using Latin terms in his arguments.

One day in court Lincoln's opponent, who was trying to impress the jury with his learning, quoted a legal maxim and then, hoping to humiliate Lincoln, turned to him and said: "That is so, is it not, Mr. Lincoln?"

"If that's Latin," Lincoln replied, "you had better call another witness."

(see SELF-DEFENSE)

LAW PARTNER

Abraham Lincoln formed a lasting friendship with his law partner William H. Herndon. Just before he left Springfield for Washington to assume the duties of the presidency, Lincoln stopped by the dingy little "Lincoln & Herndon" law office, sat down on the couch, and said to his partner:

"Billy, you and I have been together for more than twenty years and have never passed a harsh word. Will you let my name stay on the old sign until I come back from Washington?"

Tears welled up in Herndon's eyes. "Mr. Lincoln," he said, putting out his hand, "I will never have any other partner while you live."

Lincoln never returned to his law office. But the sign stayed in its place. From that day until the day Lincoln died, all the business of the firm was conducted in the name of "Lincoln & Herndon."

LAWSUIT

When Abraham Lincoln was practicing law in Springfield, Illinois, a prospective client approached him with a legal claim to six hundred dollars. But it soon became apparent that winning the claim would bankrupt a widow and impoverish her six children.

"Some things that are right legally are not right morally," said Lincoln, refusing to take the case though he was certain he could win it. "But I will give you some advice for which I will charge nothing. I advise a sprightly, energetic man like you to try your hand at making six hundred dollars in some other way."

(see LAWYERS, LEGAL FEES)

LAWYERS

As a lawyer, Abraham Lincoln was at his best in court. He loathed office work, the drafting of legal papers, and letter writing, leaving that drudgery to his law partner William H. Herndon. But when it came time to argue a case in court, Lincoln was ready. He was a formidable antagonist even when he had a weak case, and when he had right and justice on his side, he was practically unbeatable. Lincoln refused to take a case if he believed justice was on the other side; thus he was never ambivalent when he appeared before a jury. When he addressed a jury, he did so in a friendly, conversational tone, using simple words, avoiding pompous legal terms, making jurors believe that he wanted only justice and fair play. He usually summed up his argument by telling a little story that plainly illustrated the matter. If there were no precedents on his side, he would appeal to the jurors' common sense, telling them what he believed it was right for them to do and concluding with his favorite expression, "It seems to me that this ought to be the law."

Lincoln was not a crafty lawyer who relied on legal technicalities to win cases, but he was an extremely clever man nonetheless, and his disarming sense of humor helped him out of many a legal predicament. In one instance, Lincoln found himself in the peculiar position of having to plead two cases the same day before the same judge. The same principle of law was involved in both cases, but in one case Lincoln represented the defendant and in the other he represented the plaintiff.

In the morning, Lincoln made an eloquent appeal and won a dismissal for his client. In the afternoon, he appeared as a prosecutor and argued with the same zeal.

The judge, slightly amused at this about-face, called Lincoln up to the bench and asked him to account for his change of attitude.

"Your Honor," said Lincoln, "I may have been wrong this morning, but I know I'm right this afternoon."

I am not an accomplished lawyer.

—Notes for a law lecture, July 1, 1850

The leading rule for the lawyer, as for the man of every other calling, is diligence. Leave nothing for tomorrow which can be done today. Never let your correspondence fall behind.

—Notes for a law lecture, July 1, 1850

Discourage litigation. Persuade your neighbors to compromise whenever you can. . . . As a peace-maker the lawyer has a superior opportunity of being a good man. There will still be business enough.

—Notes for a law lecture, July 1, 1850

If you are resolutely determined to be a lawyer, the thing is more than half done already.

—Letter to Isham Reavis, November 5, 1855
(see BIOGRAPHY 1835–6, LATIN, LAWSUIT, LEGAL FEES, SELF DEFENSE)

LAZINESS

Abraham Lincoln as a young lad once hauled a sack of grain to a mill whose proprietor had a reputation as the laziest man in the state of Illinois. After observing the miller at work for a while, Lincoln said wearily, "I can *eat* that grain as fast as you're grinding it."

"Indeed," grumbled the miller, "and how long do you think you could keep that up?"

"Until I starve to death," was Lincoln's answer.

(see HORSE)

LEE, ROBERT E.

When General Robert E. Lee captured Harper's Ferry, President Lincoln considered it a great calamity for the Union army. As commander in chief, he called his generals on the carpet and tried to fix responsibility for this stunning defeat.

General Henry W. Halleck was summoned, but did not know where the blame lay.

"Very well," said Lincoln. "I will ask General Schenk."

General Robert C. Schenk could throw no light upon the matter, except to say that the blame was not his.

General Robert Milroy was brought into the presence of the president, and he also entered a plea of Not Guilty.

Next it was General Hooker's turn. "Fighting Joe" Hooker emphatically denied any culpability for the setback.

Finally, President Lincoln assembled all four generals in one room and said: "Gentlemen, Harper's Ferry was surrendered, and none of you, it seems, is responsible." He paced back and forth several times, then turned and faced the generals solemnly. "But I think I know who is."

"Who, Mr. President?" the distinguished generals wanted to know. "Who?"

"General Lee is responsible!" exclaimed the president. "General Lee is to blame!"

(see BLAME, ESCAPE, GENERALS)

LEGAL FEES

Abraham Lincoln did not make much money as a law-yer—he was too conscientious and honest. Daniel Webster, who once sent him a case, was amazed at the puny bill. Lincoln's fellow lawyers looked on his charges as laughably low.

On one occasion, when Lincoln's partner collected $250 for their joint services, he refused to accept his share until the fee had been reduced to what he considered fair and the overcharge had been returned to the client.

When the presiding judge of the circuit court heard about this incident, he barked, "Lincoln! Your picayune charges will impoverish the bar!"

But not all Lincoln's fees were lightweight. In one case, Lincoln and his partner William H. Herndon defended the Illinois Central Railroad in an action brought by McLean County, in August 1853, to recover taxes alleged to be due to the county. After much litigation in lower courts and two appeals to the State Supreme Court, the case was finally decided two years later in favor of the railroad company. Lincoln then went to the railroad headquarters in Chicago and presented a bill for two thousand dollars.

The railroad official balked at the bill. "Why, sir," he protested, "this is as much as Daniel Webster himself would have charged. We cannot allow such a claim. We could have hired first-class lawyers at that figure."

"We won the case, didn't we?" Lincoln demanded.

"Certainly."

"Daniel Webster, then, couldn't have done more!" Lincoln retorted angrily. He withdrew the bill, walked out of the office, and on the way home stopped at Bloomington, where he met with Grant Goodrich, Archibald Williams, Norman Judd, and several other prominent attorneys, who, on hearing of his modest fee for valuable services rendered to the railroad, persuaded him to increase the fee to five thousand dollars and agreed to testify on his behalf if he sued for that sum.

It was done. At the trial six lawyers certified that Lincoln's bill for five thousand dollars was reasonable. Judgment for that sum went by default, and the bill was paid by the railroad company.

(see LAWSUITS, LAWYERS)

LEGS

Debate was a favorite sport in Springfield, Illinois, in the 1840s, and Abraham Lincoln, the acknowledged champion of the local debating society, was often brought in to settle disputes.

One night two fellows engaged in a protracted argument, lasting several hours, over the problem of how long a man's legs should be in proportion to the size of his body. The dispute grew hotter and hotter, verging on violence and bloodshed, and since there was still no clear winner, Lincoln was called for to resolve the matter.

Lincoln arrived, listened gravely to the arguments advanced by both the contentious parties, reflected for a minute or two, and then delivered his momentous opinion:

"This question has been a source of controversy for untold ages, and it is about time it should be definitely decided," he said slowly and deliberately. "In my opinion, a man's legs should be at least long enough to reach the ground."

(see FEET)

LIBERTY

The shepherd drives the wolf from the sheep's throat, for which the sheep thanks the shepherd as his liberator, while the wolf denounces him for the same act. . . . Plainly the sheep and the wolf are not agreed upon a definition of liberty.

—Address at the Sanitary Fair, Baltimore, April 18, 1864

The world has never had a good definition of the word liberty. And the American people, just now, are much in want of one. We all declare for liberty; but in using the same word we do not all mean the same thing. With some the word liberty may mean for each man to do as he pleases with himself, and the product of his labor; while with others the same word may mean for some men to do as they please with other men, and the product of other men's labor. Here are two, not only different, but incompatible things, called by the same name, liberty. And it follows that each of the things is, by the respective parties, called by two different and incompatible names—liberty and tyranny.

—Address, Baltimore, April 18, 1864

What constitutes the bulwark of our own liberty and independence? It is not our frowning battlements, our bristling sea coasts, our army and our navy. These are not our reliance against tyranny. All of those may be turned against us without making us weaker for the struggle. Our reliance is in the love of liberty which God has planted in us. Our defense is in the spirit which prized liberty as the heritage of all men, in all lands everywhere. Destroy this spirit and you have planted the seeds of despotism at your own doors.

—Speech at Edwardsville, Illinois, September 11, 1858
(see AMERICA, DECLARATION, FREEDOM, SLAVERY)

LIBERTY POLE

The Russian ambassador, at a White House reception, was conversing with President Lincoln about national traits when the president asked, "Would you have taken me for an American if you had met me anywhere else than in this country?"

The Russian grinned at the president and, taking in his tall frame, remarked wryly, "No, I should have taken you for a Pole."

Lincoln drew himself up to his full height. "And so I am," he said, "and a Liberty Pole at that."

LINCOLN, ROBERT TODD

Abraham Lincoln's son, Robert Todd Lincoln (1843–1926), enjoyed what was perhaps the most distinguished career of any presidential progeny in U.S. history to date. After graduating from Harvard, he served in the Civil War as a captain on the staff of Ulysses S. Grant. When the war was over he attended Harvard Law School and became a corporate lawyer. In 1881 he was appointed by President James A. Garfield to be secretary of war. He served in that cabinet post until 1885. Under President Benjamin Harrison he served as U.S. minister to Great Britain from 1889 to 1893. Later he resumed his law practice and became president of the Pullman Company from 1897 to 1911, after which he was chairman of the board and director of various banks until his death in 1926.

Robert Todd Lincoln's life was crisscrossed with tragedy. It is a curious footnote to history that he was present as three different presidents lay dying from assassins' bullets. He was by his dying father's bedside in 1865; he witnessed the shooting of President Garfield in Washington, D.C., in 1881; and he was a guest at the

Exposition in Buffalo, New York, when President William McKinley was shot in 1901. He wrote laconically, "There is a certain fatality about presidential functions when I am present."

(see BIOGRAPHY 1843–6)

LINCOLN TOTEM POLE

In the year 1867 on the Tongas Island off the coast of Alaska, the Raven clan of the Tlingit Indians raised up a totem pole fifty feet high, topped by a carved figure of Abraham Lincoln.

Slavery had been common among the Tlingit Indians, particularly among the wealthy Eagle clan of the tribe. The Eagles would go on forays as far south as California and take prisoners from neighboring Indian tribes, whom they would keep or trade as slaves. Hostility developed between the Raven clan and the wealthy, slave-trafficking Eagles.

When a United States revenue cutter came to the little island in 1867 with the news of the Emancipation Proclamation of 1863 and the Thirteenth Amendment of 1865, the Ravens were inspired by the story and decided to build a totem pole to honor the Great Emancipator—and to shame the Eagles. Their artists carved Lincoln complete with his stovepipe hat. The tale of Lincoln and the freeing of the slaves was adopted as one of the permanent legends of the Raven clan, recited at tribal festivals.

Later in the year 1867 the Tlingit Indians came under the jurisdiction of the United States, as part of the provision of the Alaska Purchase. Thus all the Eagles' slaves were in fact freed by Lincoln's famous proclamation.

Today three Lincoln totem poles are still in existence. The original totem pole from Tongas was placed in a museum at Juneau. A copy was erected at Saxman,

Alaska, in 1940, and another is preserved in the Illinois State Museum in Springfield.

(see EMANCIPATION)

LION TAMING

Early in the Civil War, when the Confederates appeared to be winning, President Lincoln was advised to give up Fort Sumter and other federal properties in the southern states.

To one such adviser, W. C. Reeves of Virginia, Lincoln made this reply: "Do you remember the fable of the lion and the woodman's daughter? Well, Aesop says that a lion was very much in love with a woodman's daughter. The fair maid preferred the lion to her father. When the lion applied for the girl, the father replied: 'Your teeth are too long.' The lion went to a dentist and had them extracted. Returning, he asked again for his bride. 'No,' said the woodman. 'Your claws are too long.' Going back to the dentist, he had them drawn. Then he returned once more to claim his bride, and the woodman, seeing that he was unarmed, beat out his brains." Lincoln paused, then asked: "Would it not be so with me, if I give up all that is asked?"

(see DEFEAT, GOVERNMENT)

LITTLE WOMAN

Abraham Lincoln was sitting in the newspaper office of the *State Journal* in Springfield, Illinois, when the news arrived from the telegraph office across the street that he had been nominated for president by the Republican party at its convention in Chicago.

"Mr. Lincoln, you are nominated on the third ballot," the telegraph operator wrote on a scrap of paper.

Lincoln stared at the piece of paper silently, amid the tumultuous shouts and cheers of his friends all around him. Then he rose, tucked the piece of paper into his pocket, and said quietly, "There's a little woman down at our house who would like to hear this. I'll go down and tell her."

LOCAL INTERESTS

After Attorney General Edward Bates resigned in 1864, Lincoln's cabinet was left without a Southern member. A few days before the convening of the Supreme Court, President Lincoln sent for Titian G. Coffey, the acting Attorney General, and said: "My cabinet has shrunk up North, and I must find a Southern man."

"Is it really necessary that he be from the South, Mr. President?"

Lincoln nodded. "If the twelve apostles were to be chosen nowadays," he said, "the interest of locality would have to be heeded."

LYING

No man has a good-enough memory to make a successful liar.

—Attributed

M

MAJORITY RULE

Unanimity is impossible; the rule of a minority, as a permanent arrangement, is wholly inadmissible; so that, rejecting the majority principle, anarchy or despotism in some form is all that is left.

—First Inaugural Address, March 4, 1861
(see GOVERNMENT)

MARRIAGE

Marriage is neither heaven nor hell; it is simply purgatory.

—Attributed

I have now come to the conclusion never again to think of marrying, and for this reason: I can never be satisfied with anyone who would be blockhead enough to have me.

—Letter to Mrs. Orville Browning, April 1, 1838

My old father used to have a saying that "if you make a bad bargain, *hug* it the tighter"; and it occurs to me that if the bargain you have just closed can possibly be called a bad one, it is certainly the most *pleasant one* for applying that maxim to, which my fancy can, by any effort, picture.

—Letter to Joshua F. Speed, February 25, 1842
(on Speed's recent marriage)
(see BIOGRAPHY 1842)

MARX, KARL

Karl Marx wrote a letter to President Lincoln on January 7, 1865, offering his view of the Union victory in the Civil War as a triumph of the American working class:

"The workingmen of Europe feel sure that as the American War of Independence initiated a new era of ascendency for the middle class, so the American anti-slavery War will do for the working classes. They consider it an earnest of the epoch to come, that it fell to the lot of Abraham Lincoln, the single-minded son of the working class, to lead his country through the matchless struggle for the rescue of the enchained race and the reconstruction of a social world."

(see CLASSES, WORKERS)

MASTERS

When we were the political slaves of King George, and wanted to be free, we called the maxim that "all men are created equal" a self-evident truth, but now when we have grown fat, and have lost all dread of being slaves ourselves, we have become so greedy to be *masters* that we call the same maxim "a self-evident lie."

—Letter to George Robertson, August 15, 1855
(see DECLARATION, SLAVERY)

McCLELLAN, GENERAL GEORGE B.

During the Civil War, none of his generals caused the commander in chief more aggravation than did General George B. McClellan. On one occasion, General Mc-Clellan wrote the president a long letter pontificating about what policies to pursue.

"What did you reply?" someone asked.

"Nothing," said the president. "But it made me think of the Irishman whose horse kicked up and caught his foot in the stirrup. 'Arrah!' said the Irishman. 'If you are going to get on I will get off.' "

In the spring of 1862, when General McClellan was in command of the Union forces, there was a long lull in the action while the cautious general, anxious to avoid any costly mistakes, waged a waiting campaign.

At first President Lincoln admitted his impatience only to close friends. "General McClellan's tardiness and unwillingness to fight the enemy or follow up advantages gained," he told an intimate acquaintance, "reminds me of a man back in Illinois who knew a few law phrases but whose lawyer lacked aggressiveness. The man finally lost all patience, and springing to his feet vociferated: 'Why don't you go at him with a fi.fa., a demurrer, a capias, a surrebutter, or a *ne exeat*, or something; even a *nundam actum* or a *non est?'*

"I wish General McClellan would go at the enemy with something—I don't care what. General McClellan is a pleasant and scholarly gentleman. And he is an admirable engineer. But he seems to have a special talent for a stationary engine."

President Lincoln grew more and more exasperated at McClellan's lack of progress. "It is called the Army of the Potomac but it is only McClellan's bodyguard," he wrote in a dispatch, April 9, 1862. When his patience reached its limit, Lincoln addressed a brief letter to Mc-Clellan:

"My dear McClellan: If you are not using the army, I should like to borrow it for a while.

Yours respectfully,

A. Lincoln."

(see COWS, DIVORCE, GENERALS)

MERCY

During the Civil War, President Lincoln was asked by a lady who was prominent in Alexandria, Virginia, society to release a certain church that had been expropriated by the Union forces to serve as a hospital.

Lincoln countered by asking her why she, obviously a lady of substance, did not donate the money to build a hospital. She replied that her estates were hampered by the war and she could not afford it.

At this answer, Lincoln could not suppress a chuckle. "You, as a representative of your class in Alexandria, remind me of the story of the young man who had an aged father and mother owning considerable property. The young man being an only son, impatient for good fortune, and sincerely believing that his old parents had outlived their usefulness, assassinated them both. He was accused, tried, and convicted of the murders. When the judge came to pass sentence upon him and called upon him to give any reason he might have why the sentence of death should not be passed, the young man stood up and promptly replied that he hoped the court would have mercy upon him because he was a poor orphan!"*

METHODS

"Every man has his own peculiar and particular way of doing things," observed President Lincoln, "and he is often criticized because his way is not the one adopted by others. The great idea is to accomplish what you set out to do. When a man is successful in whatever he attempts, he has many imitators, and the methods used are not closely scrutinized, although no man who is of good intent will resort to mean, underhanded, scurvy tricks.

"That reminds me of a fellow out in Illinois who had better luck in getting prairie chickens than anyone in the neighborhood. He never seemed to exert himself, being listless and indifferent when out after game, but he always brought home all the chickens he could carry, while some of the others, with their finely trained dogs and latest improved fowling pieces, came home alone.

" 'How is it, Jake," asked one unsuccessful sportsman, who though a fine marksman came home empty-handed, 'that you never come home without an armful of birds?'

"At first Jake was reluctant to divulge a trade secret, but after persistent prodding he began to weaken. 'You'll tell,' he said, testily.

" 'I won't say a word. Honest, Jake. Hope to drop dead if I do.'

*Soviet premier Nikita Khruschev used this anecdote to define *chutspah* during his visit to the United States in 1959.

" 'Promise never to say nothing if I tell ya?'

" 'Cross my heart three times.'

"Somewhat reassured, Jake put his mouth close to the ear of his interrogator and said, in a solemn whisper, 'All you got to do is jes to hide in a fence corner an' make a noise like a turnip. That brings them chickens every time.' "

(see CRITICS)

MEXICAN WAR

Although the Mexican War was very popular, Abraham Lincoln, then a member of Congress, took a firm stand against it. He asserted that it was a war of aggression and those who claimed otherwise reminded him of the Illinois farmer who said: "I ain't greedy 'bout land. I only want what jines mine."

Skeptical of the self-righteous claims of the expansionists, Lincoln declared: "Young America is very anxious to fight for the liberation of enslaved nations and colonies, provided, always, that they have land. As to those who have no land and would be glad of help, he considers they can wait a few hundred years longer."

Wary of the wave of patriotism stirred up by the war, Lincoln remarked that even the old town loafer was caught up in the fervor.

" 'I feel patriotic,' the old fellow told me.

" 'What do you mean by that?' I asked.

" 'Why,' said the old geezer, 'when I get this way, I feel like I want to kill somebody or steal something.' "

(see MILITARY)

MIGHT

It has been said of the world's history hitherto that might makes right. It is for us and for our time to reverse the maxim and to say that right makes might.

—Attributed

MILITARY

President Lincoln was an excellent military strategist and as commander in chief he directed the Union armies and their principal campaigns, but he was careful to give credit to his generals for any victories that were achieved.

After the Battle of Gettysburg had just been fought, Lincoln sensed an opportunity to end the war by driving hard against Lee's rear in retreat. As commander in chief he ordered General George G. Meade to pursue. Then he attached the following handwritten note along with the official orders:

"The order I enclose is not of record. If you succeed, you need not publish the order. If you fail, publish it. Then, if you succeed, you will have all the credit of the movement. If not, I'll take the responsibility."

Military glory—that attractive rainbow that rises in showers of blood.

—Gross, *Lincoln's Own Story*
(see GENERALS)

MIND

Happy day, when, all appetites controlled, all passions subdued, all matters subjected, mind, all conquering mind, shall live and move the monarch of the world.

Glorious consummation! Hail fall of Fury! Reign of Reason, all hail!

—Speech, Springfield, Illinois, February 22, 1842

MINORITY

The arrest on the high seas of the Confederate Commissioners James Mason and John Slidell, forcedly removed from the British steamer *Trent*, nearly led to a war with England. Popular sentiment in the North was in favor of such a war, but President Lincoln insisted on maintaining neutral relations with England. "One war at a time," he said.

At a cabinet meeting, President Lincoln found that only one member of his cabinet supported his neutral policy toward England.

"I am reminded of a fellow out in my State of Illinois who happened to wander into a church while a revival meeting was in progress. To be truthful, this individual was not entirely sober at the time, and with that instinct which seems to impel all men in his condition to assume a prominent part in proceedings, he staggered up the aisle to the very front pew.

"Everyone in the congregation noticed his entrance, but he did not care; for a while he joined audibly in the singing, bellowing 'Amen' at the close of the prayers, but drowsiness overtook him in the middle of the sermon, and he dozed off to sleep. Before the meeting closed, the pastor asked the usual question—'Who are on the Lord's side?'—and the congregation arose en masse, except for the vagrant. When the pastor asked, 'Who are on the side of the Devil?' the sleeper was just waking up. He heard a portion of the interrogatory, and, seeing the minister on his feet, arose.

" 'I don't exactly understand the question,' he said, 'but I'll stand by you, parson, to the last. But between you and me,' he added, glancing around the church, 'it seems that we're in a hopeless minority.'

"Well, I'm in a hopeless minority now," said President Lincoln with a wink at his supporter, "and I'll just have to admit it." ·

(see AYES)

MISSISSIPPI

The Father of Waters again goes unvexed to the sea.

—Letter to James C. Conkling, August 26, 1863
(on the reopening of the Mississippi River
during Civil War)

MOB

There is no grievance that is a fit object of redress by mob law.

—Address at the Young Men's Lyceum, January 27, 1838
(see VIOLENCE)

MODERATION

In grave emergencies, moderation is generally safer than radicalism.

—Quoted in *Lincoln Encyclopedia*

MONEY

I have news from Ottawa that we *win* our Galatin & Saline County case. As the Dutch Justice said when he married folks, "Now vere is my hundred tollars?"

—Letter to Andrew McCallen, July 4, 1851

The plainest print cannot be read through a gold eagle.

—Speech, Springfield, Illinois, June 26, 1857

MORALITY

With malice toward none, with charity for all, with firmness in the right, as God gives us to see the right.

—Second Inaugural Address, March 4, 1865
(see RIGHT AND WRONG)

MOTHER

All that I am or hope to be, I owe to my angel mother.

—Attributed
(see BIOGRAPHY 1809)

MOTIVATION

When President Lincoln was informed that one of the members of his cabinet was working behind the scenes to secure a presidential nomination for himself in 1864, the president was amused rather than annoyed.

"A friend and I were once plowing corn," he recounted, "I driving the horse and he holding the plow. The horse was lazy and moved with great reluctance, if at all, until suddenly once without warning he galloped across the field so fast that I, with my long legs, could scarcely keep up with him. On reaching the end of the furrow, I found an enormous chin-fly fastened upon him, and knocked him off. My friend asked me what I did that for. I told him I hated to see the old horse bitten so. 'But, Abe,' said my friend, 'that's all that made him go.'

"Now," Lincoln concluded, "if our colleague has a

presidential chin-fly biting him, I'm not going to knock him off, if it will only make his department go."

(see CABINET)

MOVING

When Abe Lincoln first arrived in Springfield, Illinois, to begin his career as a lawyer, he brought with him all his possessions in the world, consisting of three law books and a few articles of clothing, all of which fit into a pair of saddlebags.

Discovering that a single bed would cost him seventeen dollars, he was obliged to look for lodgings elsewhere. "It is probably cheap enough, but I do not have enough money to pay for it."

A newfound friend named Joshua Speed, a local merchant, offered to front the money.

Lincoln declined. "If I fail here as a lawyer, I will probably never pay you at all."

Then Speed offered to share a large double bed with him.

"Where is your room?" asked Lincoln.

"Upstairs," said Speed.

Without saying a word, Lincoln took his saddlebags on his arm, walked upstairs, set them down on the floor, came back downstairs again, and with a face beaming with satisfaction, exclaimed: "Well, Speed, I'm moved!"

(see POVERTY)

N

NIAGARA FALLS

It calls up the indefinite past. When Columbus first
sought this continent—when Christ suffered on the
cross—when Moses led Israel through the Red Sea—nay,
even when Adam first came from the hand of his Maker;
then, as now, Niagara was roaring here. The eyes of
that species of extinct giants whose bones fill the
mounds of America have gazed on Niagara, as ours do
now. Contemporary with the first race of men, and older
than the first man, Niagara is strong and fresh today as
ten thousand years ago. The Mammoth and Mastodon,
so long dead that fragments of their monstrous bones
alone testify that they ever lived, have gazed on Niagara—in that long, long time never still for a single moment, never froze, never slept, never rested.

> —From an article on Niagara Falls found in Lincoln's
> posthumous papers
> (see CRITICS)

NOISE

Abraham Lincoln was a quiet man who rarely raised his voice, and he disliked persons who spoke loudly and excitedly when they were trying to persuade him of their point of view.

"Volume adds nothing to credibility," he said. "These noisy people remind me of an incident that occurred out in Illinois while I was practicing, or trying to practice, some law there. I will say, though, that I practiced a good deal more law than I ever got paid for. But that is beside the point.

"A fellow who lived just outside town, on the bank of a large marsh, conceived of a big idea in the money-making line. He took it to a prominent merchant and pitched his proposal. 'There are at least ten million frogs in that marsh near me, an' I'll just arrest a couple of carloads of them an' hand them over to you. You can send them to the big cities and make lots of money for both of us. Frogs' legs are a great delicacy in the big towns, you know, an' not very plentiful. It won't take me more'n two or three days to catch 'em. They make so much damn noise my family can't sleep nohow, and by this deal I figure I'll get rid of a nuisance and gather in some cash.'

"The merchant was impressed by this plan and agreed to pay the fellow well for the two carloads of frogs. Two days passed, then three, a week went by, then two weeks were gone before the fellow showed up again, carrying a small basket. He looked weary to the bone and wasn't talkative a bit. He just threw down the basket on the counter and said, 'There's your frogs.'

" 'You haven't got two carloads in that basket, have you?' said the merchant, with his arms folded.

" 'No,' said the frog hunter, 'and there ain't no two

carloads to be got. There ain't two carloads of frogs in this whole blasted world.'

" 'But I thought you said there were at least ten million of them in that marsh,' recalled the merchant. 'You calculated it according to the noise they made.'

" 'Well,' said the fellow, 'accordin' to the noise they made, there was, I figured, a hundred million of 'em, but when I had waded and swum that there marsh day and night fer two blessed weeks, I couldn't harvest but six. There's still two or three left yet, an' the marsh is 'most as noisy as it uster be. We haven't catched up on any of our lost sleep yet, neither. But you can have these here six, an' I won't charge you a cent fer 'em.'

"And just like the frogs in that marsh," said the president, "these boisterous people make too much noise in proportion to their numbers."

(see EXAGGERATION)

OATH

I take the official oath today with no mental reserva-
tions, and with no purpose to construe the Constitution
by any hypocritical rules.

—First Inaugural Address, March 4, 1861

You can have no oath registered in heaven to destroy
the government; while I shall have the most solemn one
to "preserve, protect, and defend" it.

—First Inaugural Address, March 4, 1861

OFFICE SEEKERS

"Mr. President," said the spokesman for a group of Republicans who came to press for a port-collectorship for
their man, "our distinguished colleague is preeminently
qualified, not only by his administrative capacity, but by
his invincible loyalty to Republican principles. No hon-

ors, sir, could be showered on him that could elevate him higher in the estimation of his fellow-men."

"Gentlemen," replied President Lincoln, "it gratifies me to hear such high praise so justly bestowed. You are right, Mr. Chairman, no honors could be showered on him that would elevate him higher in the estimation of his fellow-man. Such a man needs no office; it could bring him no additional advantage. To appoint so good and excellent a gentleman to a paltry place like this would be an act of injusice to him. I shall reserve the office for some poor politician who needs it."

(see APPLICANTS, HAWAII, JACKASS)

OPEN-MINDEDNESS

I shall try to correct errors when shown to be errors, and I shall adopt new views so fast as they shall appear to be true views.

—Letter to Horace Greeley, August 22, 1862
(see CONSERVATISM, PAST)

PAPER MONEY

Paper money as we know it in the United States today was initiated during Abraham Lincoln's administration. In the midst of the Civil War, when the nation was relying mainly on metal money, there was a severe financial crisis. The president was unable to come up with enough coinage to pay the troops. Urged by some of his advisers to print paper money, Lincoln arranged a conference between them and Treasury Secretary Salmon P. Chase, who angrily asserted that it would be unconstitutional to print paper money.

The next day, President Lincoln sent his aides back to the Treasury Department with this note for Chase: "You take care of the Treasury and I will take care of the Constitution."

Paper money has been part of American life ever since.

(see CABINET)

PARDON

During the Civil War, President Lincoln was besieged with appeals for pardons for soldiers caught in the machinery of military discipline. Such appeals were usually supported by letters from influential people. One day Lincoln found on his desk a single sheet of paper—an appeal from a soldier without any supporting documents.

"What? Has this man no friends?" exclaimed the president.

"No, sir," said the adjutant, "not one."

Lincoln sighed. "Then I will be his friend."

(see COURT MARTIAL, HANDSOME, REPRIEVE)

PAST

The dogmas of the quiet past are inadequate to the stormy present.

—Second Annual Message to Congress, 1862
(see CONSERVATISM, OPEN-MINDEDNESS)

PATIENCE

A man watches his pear tree day after day, impatient for the ripening of fruit. Let him attempt to *force* the process, and he may spoil both fruit and tree. But let him patiently *wait*, and the ripe fruit at length falls into his lap.

—Attributed

PEOPLE

President Lincoln, mingling with a crowd of plain-looking people, overheard someone comment on his appearance: "That is the president of the United States? But he is such a common-looking man!"

Lincoln spoke up. "Common people are the best in the world: that is the reason the Lord makes so many of them."

(see COMMON MAN)

Why should there not be a patient confidence in the ultimate justice of the people? Is there any better or equal hope in the world?

—First Inaugural Address, March 4, 1861

While the people retain their virtue and vigilance, no administration, by any extreme of wickedness or folly, can very seriously injure the government in the short space of four years.

—First Inaugural Address, March 4, 1861

Let the people know the truth and the country is safe.

—Attributed
(see DEMOCRACY, GOVERNMENT, RIGHTS)

PERFECTION

It is said in one of the admonitions of the Lord, "As your Father in Heaven is perfect, be ye also perfect." The Savior, I suppose, did not expect that any human creature could be perfect as the Father in Heaven. . . . He set that up as a standard, and he who did most toward reaching that standard attained the highest degree of moral perfection.

—Speech, Chicago, Illinois, July 10, 1858
(see HUMAN NATURE, MORALITY)

PERSEVERANCE

Hold on with a bulldog grip, and chew and choke as much as possible.

—Telegram to General Ulysses S. Grant, August 17, 1864
(at the siege of Petersburgh)

PERSUASION

If you would win a man to your cause, first convince him that you are his true friend. Therein is a drop of honey that catches his heart, which, say what he will, is the greatest highroad to his reason, and which when once gained, you will find but little trouble in convincing his judgment of the justice of your cause, if, indeed, that cause be really a just one. On the contrary, assume to dictate to his judgment, or to command his action, or to make him as one to be shunned or despised, and he will retreat within himself, close all the avenues to his head and heart; and though your cause be naked truth itself, transformed to the heaviest lance, harder than steel and sharper than steel can be made, and though you throw it with more than Herculean force and precision, you shall be no more able to pierce him than to penetrate the hard shell of a tortoise with a rye straw.

—Attributed

PHANTOM FUNERAL TRAIN

Abraham Lincoln, the first president to be assassinated, haunts America more than any other president. He haunts the imagination of his countrymen, and according to a story told by employees of the New York Central Railroad, he haunts the train tracks.

It is a folk legend in the railroad business that every

year on April 27 Lincoln's funeral train rides the rails once again. First in the procession is an engine with grinning skeletons manning the controls inside the cab and a spectral band playing dirges. Then comes the funeral car carrying Lincoln's flag-draped coffin, followed by a third car filled with men in blue coats. When Lincoln's phantom funeral train passes by, according to the legend, all clocks and watches stop.

(see DREAM)

PHOTOGRAPH

Photographs of Abraham Lincoln often showed him solemn-faced, without a hint of his famous sense of humor. Presenting a sad-looking photograph of himself to some Coles County relatives, he said, apologetically, "This is not a very good-looking picture; but it's the best that could be produced from the poor subject."

(see HOMELINESS, PORTRAIT)

PIETY

Two attractive ladies from Tennessee called at the White House one day and begged the president to release their husbands, who were rebel prisoners at Johnson's Island. One of the ladies advanced the pious argument that her husband was a deeply religious man and should be released for that reason.

Lincoln was skeptical. "Madam, you say your husband is a religious man. Perhaps I am not a good judge of these things, but in my opinion the religion that makes men rebel and fight against a just government in defense of an unjust institution that makes slaves of men whom God made free is not the genuine article. The religion that reconciles men to the idea of eating their bread in the sweat of other men's faces is not the kind to get to heaven on."

In the end the president ordered the men to be released, not before he told the ladies, with impressive solemnity, that he expected them to subdue the rebellious spirit of their husbands and that he thought they would do well to reform their religious practices.

"True patriotism," said Lincoln, "is more holy than false piety."

(see CHRISTIANITY, RELIGION)

PLACEMENT

Placing the right person in the right place is one of the greatest challenges of any chief executive. There was a time during the Civil War when General John C. Frémont—the noted western explorer, soldier, and Republican—was without a command. One day in discussing the Fremont problem with Congressman George Julian, President Lincoln remarked that the situation reminded him of the old man who advised his son to take a wife, to which the son replied: "All right, Dad. Whose wife shall I take?"

PLANNING

If we could first know where we are, and whither we are tending, we could then better judge what to do, and how to do it.

—Speech, Springfield, Illinois, June 16, 1858

POLITICS

My politics are short and sweet, like the old woman's dance.

—Attributed

I have not permitted myself, gentlemen, to conclude that I am the best man in the country, but I am reminded in this connection of an old Dutch farmer who remarked that it was not best to swap horses while crossing a stream.

—Reply to National Union League on notification of his renomination, June 9, 1864
(see PRESIDENCY)

PORTRAIT

The day after he was renominated for the presidency at the Baltimore convention in 1864, Lincoln received a visit from the Philadelphia delegation, whose members came to pay their respects.

The chairman of the delegation introduced one of the members thus: "Mr. President, this is Mr. Smiley of the second district of our state, a most earnest friend of yours and our cause. He has, among other things, been good enough to paint, and donate to our league rooms, a most beautiful portrait of yourself."

President Lincoln grasped Smiley's hand, shook it cordially, and said with a grin, "I presume, sir, in painting your beautiful portrait, you took your idea of my form from my principles and not from my person."

(see HANDSOME, HOMELINESS, PHOTOGRAPH)

POSTERITY

Few can be induced to labor exclusively for posterity.
Posterity has done nothing for us.

—Speech to Springfield Washington Temperance
Society, February 22, 1842
(see LABOR)

POSTPONEMENT

An old man begged President Lincoln to pardon his son.

"I am sorry," said Lincoln, sadly, "but I can do nothing for you. Listen to this telegram I received from General Butler yesterday: 'President Lincoln, I pray you not to interfere with the courts-martial of the army. You will destroy all discipline among our soldiers.' "

Tears welled up in the old man's eyes.

Lincoln's heart melted. "By jingo!" he cried. "Butler or no Butler, here goes!" He wrote out an order and showed it to the father: "Job Smith is not to be shot until further orders from me—A. Lincoln."

The elder Smith was not cheered by this. "But you might order him to be shot next week."

"My friend," replied President Lincoln, "I see you are not very acquainted with me. If your son never dies until orders come from me to shoot him, he will live to be a great deal older than Methuselah."

(see PARDON)

POSTURE

Abraham Lincoln volunteered for the Illinois militia during the Black Hawk Indian War of 1832. His colonel, a short man merely five feet tall, was offended by the poor posture of the six foot four inch Lincoln.

"Come on, Lincoln," the little colonel snapped at the slouching giant, "hold your head high!"

"Yes, sir." Abe straightened his back and stood tall.

"Higher!"

Lincoln stretched his neck taut toward the sky, "Just so, sir?"

"Yes, but a little higher!"

Lincoln strained and stood taller still. "And am I always to remain so?"

"Yes, Lincoln, always!"

"Then," said Abe sadly, "goodbye, Colonel, for I shall never see you again!"

(see FEET)

POVERTY

Abraham Lincoln had a good deal of feeling for the poor, for he was well acquainted with poverty himself. When once asked to tell the story of his early life, he replied: "It is contained in one line of Gray's 'Elegy in a Country Churchyard'—'The short and simple annals of the poor.' "

(see MOVING)

POWER

It's a good rule never to send a mouse to catch a skunk or a polliwog to tackle a whale.

—Attributed

PRAYER

"I have been driven many times to my knees, by the overwhelming conviction that I had nowhere else to go. My own wisdom and that of all about me seemed insufficient for that day." Lincoln often resorted to prayer.

He regarded the Civil War, in some respects, as a divine punishment visited upon the United States for its accumulated national sins. He also saw it as an opportunity to purge the nation of some of those sins forever and to achieve a national salvation. Taking office at the beginning of the war, he offered this prayer for the nation:

> We have been the recipients of the choicest bounties of Heaven. We have been preserved these many years in peace and prosperity. We have grown in numbers, wealth, and power as no other nation has ever grown—but we have forgotten God!
>
> We have forgotten the gracious hand that preserved us in peace, and multiplied and enriched, and strengthened us; and we have vainly imagined, in the deceitfulness of our hearts, that all these blessings were produced by some superior wisdom and virtue of our own.
>
> Intoxicated with unbroken success, we have become too self-sufficient to feel the necessity of redeeming grace, too proud to pray to the God that made us.
>
> It behooves us, then, to humble ourselves before the offended Power, to confess our national sins, and to pray for clemency and forgiveness.
>
> I still have confidence that the Almighty, the Maker of the universe, will, through the instrumentality of this great and intelligent people, bring us through present difficulties as He has through all the other difficulties of our country.

(see CIVIL WAR, GOD)

PREACHING

When I hear a man preach, I like to see him act as if he were fighting bees.

—Attributed

PREDETERMINATION

There was a time during the Civil War in 1862 when Washington, D.C., was left relatively unprotected while the Union armies were all concentrated elsewhere. Lincoln was uneasy knowing that the nation's capital was defended by only fifteen hundred men, two big guns, and an old sloop of war.

When he expressed concern to General Winfield Scott, who was in charge of the fifteen hundred troops, the general tried to reassure him. "It has been ordained, Mr. President, that the city shall not be captured by the Confederates."

The president replied, "Even if it has been ordained, I would feel easier if the city were better protected. This reminds me of the old trapper out in the West who had been assured by the city folks who hired him as a guide that all important matters regarding life and death were prearranged."

" 'It is ordained,' said one of the party to the old trapper, 'that you are to die at a certain time, and no one can kill you before that time. If you met a thousand Indians, and your death had not been ordained for that day, you would escape, for a certainty.'

" 'Aw, I don't understand this "ordained" business,' the trapper replied. 'I don't care to run no extra risks. I always have my gun with me, so that if I come across some reds I can feel sure that I won't cross the Jordan without takin' a few of them pagans with me. Now, what would happen, for instance, if I met an Indian in

the woods; he drew a bead on me—suppos'n, now, that
he wasn't more'n ten feet away—an' I didn't have nothing to protect myself; sayin' if the redskin was dead
ready to kill me now—well, even if it was ordained that
the Indian (sayin' he was a good shot), was to die that
very minute, an' I wasn't, what would I do then without my gun?'

"That's how it is, Scott," said President Lincoln.
"Even if it has been ordained that the city of Washington will never be taken by the Confederates, what if
they don't know that? What would we do, without ad-
equate men and heavy guns, if they made a serious assault on the city?"

PRESIDENCY

Just before taking the oath of office, Abraham Lincoln
met the outgoing President James Buchanan, who said
to him, "If you are as happy, my dear sir, on entering
this house as I am in leaving it and returning home, you
are the happiest man in this country."

Before long, Lincoln knew what Jefferson called the
"splendid misery" of the presidency. "I have been told
I was on the road to hell," said Lincoln, "but I had no
idea it was just a mile down the road with a Dome on
it."

The responsibilities of a president are awesome, while
the ceremonies are often irksome. On top of all the glory
is heaped a heavy helping of harsh criticism. But no
president ever had to bear more abuse than did Lincoln,
who presided over a divided nation. And not all the
invective came from the South. One New York newspaper, for example, referred to him as "that hideous
baboon at the other end of the avenue" and asserted
that "Barnum should buy and exhibit him as a zoolog-
ical curiosity." Lincoln was called a buffoon, an ape, a

clown, a tyrant, a usurper, a monster, an idiot, a eu-
nuch, a bigot, a demagogue, an atheist, a blunderer, a
bully, a Judas Iscariot, a Nero, a charlatan, a joker, and
an ugly fool. Asked whether he was ever wearied by
the nation's highest office, Lincoln replied, "Yes, sometimes. In fact, I feel sometimes like a man who was rid-
den out of town on a rail and said: 'If it wasn't for the
honor of the thing, I'd rather walk!' "

Nobody has ever expected me to be president. In my
poor, lean, lank face nobody has ever seen that any cab-
bages were sprouting.

—Speech against Stephen A. Douglas, July 17, 1858

I happen, temporarily, to occupy this White House. I
am a living witness that any one of your children may
look to come here as my father's child has.

—Address to Ohio soldiers, August 2, 1864

As the president in the Administration of the Government, I hope to be man enough not to know one citizen
of the United States from another, nor one section from
another.

—Reply to the Massachusetts Delegation, March 5, 1861

Should my Administration prove to be a very wicked
one, or what is more probable, a very foolish one, if
you, the people, are but true to yourselves and to the
Constitution, there is but little harm I can do, *thank God!*

—First Inaugural Address, March 4, 1861

I cannot run this thing on the theory that every office-
holder must think I am the greatest man in the nation,
and I will not.

—Lamon, *Reminiscences of Abraham Lincoln, 1847–1865*

The position is not an easy one; and the occupant, whoever he may be for the next four years, will have little leisure to pluck a thorn or plant a rose in his own pathway.

—Lamon, *Reminiscences of Abraham Lincoln, 1847–1865*
(see AMBITION, GOVERNMENT)

PRINCIPLES

Important principles may and must be inflexible.

—from Lincoln's last public address,
Washington, D.C., April 11, 1865

I intend no modification of my oft-expressed personal wish that all men, everywhere, could be free.

—Letter to Horace Greeley, August 22, 1862

PROGRESS

I shall go just so fast and only so fast as I think I'm right and the people are ready for the step.

—To Horace Maynard, in Herndon and Weik,
Herndon's Life of Lincoln

PROMOTION

There was a time when the Union generals appeared to be more concerned with jockeying for promotion than with defeating the Confederates. When President Lincoln become aware of the "wire-pulling" of certain officers to prevent the promotion of their fellow officers, he was disturbed.

Matters came to a head when the name of one particularly unpopular general was sent to the Senate for confirmation. The nomination was opposed by almost everyone in Washington. Even generals who hated each other were united in their efforts to bring every possible influence upon the Senate to prevent the general's confirmation.

"I have never been privy to the spectacle of such unanimity before," remarked President Lincoln to a delegation of lobbyists against the nomination. "You remind me of the visit a certain governor paid to the penitentiary of his state. It had been announced that the governor would hear the story of each inmate of the institution, and was prepared to rectify, either by commutation or pardon, any wrongs that had been done to any prisoner.

"One by one the convicts appeared before His Excellency, and each one steadfastly maintained that he was an innocent man, who had been sent to prison because the police didn't like him, or his friends and relatives wanted his property, or he was too popular, etc., etc. The last prisoner to appear was an individual who was not at all prepossessing. His face was against him; his eyes were shifty and suspicious-looking; he didn't have the appearance of an honest man, and he didn't act like one.

" 'Well,' said the governor, impatiently, 'I suppose you're innocent like the rest of these fellows?'

" 'No, Governor,' was the unexpected reply. 'I was guilty of the crime they charged against me, and I got just what I deserved.'

"When he had partially recovered from his astonishment, the governor drew in a deep breath, looked the prisoner squarely in the face, and said with gravity: 'I'll have to pardon you, because I don't want to leave so bad a man as you are in the company of such innocent sufferers as I have discovered your fellow-convicts to be. You might corrupt them.' And so the governor ordered the prisoner to be released.

"You gentlemen," the president concluded, "ought

to be glad that a man so bad as you represent this officer to be is to get his promotion, for then you won't be forced to associate with him any longer and suffer the contamination of his presence. I will do all I can to have the Senate confirm him.''

The nomination was confirmed.

(see GENERALS)

PROPERTY

Property is the fruit of labor; property is desirable; is a positive good in the world.

—Reply to the New York Workingmen's Association, March 21, 1864

Let not him who is houseless pull down the house of another, but let him labor diligently and build one for himself, thus, by example, assuring that his own shall be safe from violence when built.

—Reply to the New York Workingmen's Association, March 21, 1864
(see ENTERPRISE, LABOR, SELF-GOVERNMENT, WORKERS)

PROTECTION

In 1862 President Lincoln received a visit from a delegation of New York millionaires who were concerned about the threat of naval attack and asked that he furnish a gunboat for the protection of New York harbor.

Lincoln listened patiently, then replied: "Gentlemen, as you know, the credit of the government is at a very low ebb just now; greenbacks are not worth more than forty or fifty cents on the dollar; it is impossible for me, in the midst of the current crisis, to furnish you a gunboat. In fact, gentlemen, if I was worth half as much as you, and was half as worried as you seem to be, I would build a gunboat and give it to the government.''

(see BANKERS, MERCY)

PUBLIC OPINION

Public opinion in this country is everything.

—Speech at Columbus, Ohio, September 16, 1859

In this and like communities, public sentiment is everything. With public sentiment, nothing can fail. Without it, nothing can succeed.

—Speech, Ottawa, Illinois, July 31, 1858

He who moulds public sentiment goes deeper than he who enacts statutes or pronounces decisions. He makes statutes and decisions possible or impossible to be executed.

—Speech, Ottawa, Illinois, July 31, 1858

PUBLIC SPEAKING

Don't shoot too high. Aim low, and the common people will understand you.

—Attributed
(see GETTYSBURG ADDRESS)

PUNISHMENT

An applicant for office, A. J. Bleeker, was introduced to the president and was about to hand him vouching papers when President Lincoln requested that he read them aloud. With barely a blush Bleeker commenced reading his vouchers, which were full of unstinting praise.

Bleeker had not read very far when Lincoln held up a hand. "Stop a minute!" he said. "You remind me of the man who killed the dog. In fact, you are just like him."

"In what way?" asked Bleeker, suspecting that he had not received a compliment.

"Well," Lincoln replied, "this man had made up his mind to kill his dog, an ugly brute who had bitten several schoolchildren, and so he proceeded to beat out the animal's brains with a club. He continued striking the dog after the dog had been dead for some time, until a friend interrupted him, protesting, 'You needn't strike him any more; the dog is dead; you killed him at the first blow.'

" 'Oh, yes, I know,' said the fellow, 'but I believe in punishment after death.'

"And so, I see, do you," concluded President Lincoln. He gave Bleeker the appointment.

(see FLATTERY)

PUNS

Like most humorists, Abraham Lincoln could not resist the temptation to indulge in an occasional pun. Once when he was gazing out the window of his law office in Springfield, Illinois, he saw a plump and stately matron, wearing a plumed hat, making her way gingerly across the muddy street. Suddenly she slipped and fell back on her buttocks. "Reminds me of a duck," he told his law partner, who was standing beside him.

"How so?" asked his partner.

"Feathers on her head," said Lincoln, "and down on her behind."

(see ENDS, HUMOR)

QUALIFICATIONS

Hearing that a general who was supporting General George B. McClellan's presidential candidacy had been relieved of his command, President Lincoln countermanded the order. "Supporting General McClellan for the presidency is no violation of army regulations," stated Lincoln. He added: "And as a question of taste in choosing between him and me—well, I'm the longest, but he's better looking."

(see FREEDOM OF SPEECH, MCCLELLAN)

QUARRELING

It was President Lincoln's duty to deliver an official reprimand to a young officer who had been court-martialed for quarreling with an officer of higher rank.

"Quarrel not at all," wrote the president. "No man resolved to make the most of himself can spare time for personal contention. Still less can he afford to take all the consequences, including the vitiating of his temper and the loss of self-control. Yield larger things to which you can show no more than equal rights, and yield lesser ones, though clearly your own.

"Better give your path to a dog than be bitten by him in contesting for the right. Even killing the dog would not cure the bite."

(see ANGER)

R

RAISINS

The telegraph office at the War Department occupied three rooms, one of which was called "the president's room" because, in a time when telegrams provided the timeliest news, the president spent a good deal of his time there.

The chief of the telegraph office, A. B. Chandler, recalled that President Lincoln would read all the telegrams received for the heads of the different departments of government. Lincoln kept one copy of each telegram.

"President Lincoln's copies were kept in what we called the 'President's drawer' of the 'cipher desk,' " Chandler recollected. "He would come in at any time of the night or day, and go at once to this drawer, and take out a file of telegrams, and begin at the top of the stack to read them.

"He had a habit of sitting frequently on the edge of his chair, with his right knee dragged down to the floor.

I remember a curious expression of his when he got to the bottom of the new telegrams and began on those that he had read before. It was, 'Well, I guess I have got down to the raisins.'

"The first two or three times he said this he made no explanation, and I did not ask one. But one day, after he made the remark, he looked up under his eyebrows at me with a funny twinkle in his eyes, and said:

" 'I used to know a little girl out West who sometimes was inclined to eat too much. One day she ate a good many more raisins than was good for her, and followed them down with a quantity of other goodies. Sure enough, she got very sick. At last the raisins began to come up. The little girl gasped and looked at her mother and said, "Well, I will be better now, for I have got down to the raisins." ' "

READING

When Abraham Lincoln was a boy, his family owned but a handful of books. To read and improve himself, Lincoln had to walk many miles to borrow books from friends and neighbors. After his day's work on the farm was done, he would put a fresh log in the fireplace, take out a book, and read by the flickering firelight, late into the night, until he fell asleep and dreamed of greater days to come.

(see BOOKS, BIOGRAPHY 1835–6)

REFERENCE

A business firm, which was considering hiring a young attorney with whom Abraham Lincoln had been acquainted, wrote to Lincoln for a reference about the young man, asking for an honest appraisal of his potential value as an employee.

Lincoln wrote back: "He is young and ambitious, but hasn't much experience yet. He has a wife and baby; together they ought to be worth $500,000 to any man. He has an office in the Blackstone block; a small library, worth $50; a table and two chairs, $5 will cover them; and in the southeast corner of the room is a rat hole that will bear looking into."

RELIGION

Asked about his religion, Abraham Lincoln once remarked that his religion was very much like that of an old man named Glenn in Indiana, whom he heard speak at a church meeting and who said: "When I do good I feel good; when I do bad I feel bad; and that's my religion."

(see CONSCIENCE, FLOWERS, GOD, MORALITY)

REPRIEVE

A young Kentucky man who deserted the Confederate army and returned home was later arrested by a Union officer, and after a military trial, condemned to hang as a rebel spy.

A Kentucky friend of President Lincoln tried to use his personal influence with the president to obtain a reprieve.

"Yes, I understand," said the president with a sigh. "Someone has been crying, and worked upon your feelings, and now you have come here to work upon mine."

The friend then assured Lincoln of his sincere belief

in the young man's innocence. Lincoln was still not fully convinced, but he said thoughtfully:

"If I must err, I would prefer to err on the side of mercy. If a man had more than one life, I think a little hanging would not harm this one. But once he is dead we cannot bring him back, no matter how sorry we may be; so this boy shall be pardoned."

A reprieve was granted immediately.

(see COURT-MARTIAL, HANDSOME, PARDON)

REPUBLICANISM

No man is good enough to govern another man, *without that other's consent*. I say this is the leading principle—the sheet anchor of American Republicanism.

—Speech, Peoria, Illinois, October 16, 1854
(see GOVERNMENT, PEOPLE)

RESIGNATION

One day at the White House a friend of President Lincoln said something critical of a certain general. "He isn't worth the powder and ball necessary to kill him," remarked the friend. "So I have heard military men say."

"You wrong him," said the president. "He is a really great man—a philosopher. For he has mastered that ancient and wise admonition, 'know thyself.' He has formed an intimate acquaintance with himself, knows as well for what he is fitted and unfitted as any man living. Without doubt he is a remarkable man. This war has not produced another like him. Greatly to my relief, and to the interest of the country, he has resigned."

(see AVERAGE, GENERALS)

RESPONSIBILITY

You can't escape the responsibility of tomorrow by evading it today.

—Attributed

REVOLUTION

If by the mere force of numbers a majority should deprive a minority of any clearly written constitutional right, it might, in a moral point of view, justify revolution—certainly would if such a right were a vital one.

—First Inaugural Address, March 4, 1861

Any people anywhere, being included and having the power, have the *right* to rise up, and shake off the existing government, and form a new one that suits them better. This is a most valuable, a most sacred right—a right, which we hope and believe, is to liberate the world.

—Speech to the House of Representatives, January 12, 1848

Be not deceived. Revolutions do not go backward.

—Speech, May 19, 1856
(see GOVERNMENT, MAJORITY RULE, RIGHTS)

RICHMOND

In the middle of the Civil War a gentleman requested of President Lincoln a special pass that would allow him to visit Richmond, the Confederate capital.

"I would be very happy to oblige you," answered Lincoln, "if my passes were respected. But the fact is, sir, I have, within the past two years, given passes to two hundred and fifty thousand men to go to Richmond, and not one has got there yet."

RIDDLE

Lincoln liked to present this riddle to friends and acquaintances: "If three pigeons sit on a fence and you shoot and kill one of them, how many will be left?"

The answer usually given was, "Two, of course."

To which Lincoln replied: "No, there won't, for the other two will fly away."

RIDICULE

I have endured a great deal of ridicule without much malice; and have received a great deal of kindness, not quite free from ridicule. I am used to it.

—Letter to James H. Hackett, November 2, 1863

RIGHT AND WRONG

It is the eternal struggle between these two principles—right and wrong—throughout the world. They are the two principles that have stood face to face from the beginning of time; and will ever continue to struggle. The one is the common right of humanity, and the other the divine right of kings. It is the same principle in whatever shape it develops itself. It is the same spirit that says, "You toil and work and earn bread, and I'll eat it." No matter in what shape it comes, whether from the mouth of a king who seeks to bestride the people of his own nation and live by the fruit of their labor, or from one race of men as an apology for enslaving another race, it is the same tyrannical principle.

—Reply, seventh and last joint debate
with Stephen A. Douglas
(Alton, Illinois, October 15, 1858)
(see EVILS, SLAVERY)

RIGHTS

This country, with its institutions, belongs to the people who inhabit it. Whenever they shall grow weary of the existing government, they can exercise their constitutional right of amending it, or their revolutionary right to dismember or overthrow it.

—First Inaugural Address, March 4, 1861
(see GOVERNMENT, PEOPLE, REVOLUTION)

RISKS

President Lincoln's cabinet had come to the conclusion that a war with England and France was unavoidable. Both Secretary of War Edwin M. Stanton and Secretary of State William H. Seward insisted that the United States could not afford to appear to back down in the current diplomatic crisis.

"Why take any more chances than are absolutely necessary?" asked President Lincoln, who was less afraid of humiliation than of war.

"We must maintain our honor at any cost!" declared Secretary Seward.

"We would be branded as cowards before the entire world," affirmed Secretary Stanton.

"We already have one war," said President Lincoln. "One or two more are no cheaper in the bargain. And why run the greater risk when we can take a smaller one? The less risk we run, the better for us. That reminds me of the story of a hero who was on the firing line during a recent battle, in which the bullets were flying thick and furious. Finally, his courage gave way entirely, and throwing down his gun, he ran for dear life.

"As he was flying across the field at top speed, he came across an officer who drew his revolver and shouted, 'Go back to your regiment at once or I will shoot you!'

" 'Go ahead and shoot!' the racer retorted. 'What's one bullet to a whole hatful?' "

(see MEXICAN WAR)

RUNNING

A certain congressman had lent some of his leadership to the Union troops at Bull Run in July 1861, and when the Union troops were thrashed by the Confederates, the congressman took the lead in the hasty retreat back to Washington.

"I never knew but one fellow who could run like that," Lincoln would joke about it later. "He was a young man out of Illinois who had been sparking a girl much against the wishes of her father. In fact, the old man took such a dislike to him that he threatened to shoot him if he ever caught him on the premises again. One evening the young man learned that the girl's father had gone to the city, and he ventured out to the house. He was sitting in the parlor with his arm around the girl's waist and then he suddenly spied the old man coming around the corner of the house with a shotgun. Leaping through the window into the garden, he started down the path at the top of his speed like greased lightning. Just then a jackrabbit jumped up in the path in front of him. In about two leaps the boy overtook the rabbit. Giving it a kick that sent it high in the air, he yelled, 'Git out of the road, gosh dern you, and let somebody run that knows how!' "

(see BRAGGING, BULL RUN)

RUTLEDGE, ANNE

Abraham Lincoln's first love, and perhaps the greatest love of his life, was Anne Rutledge. The daughter of one of the founders of New Salem, Illinois, she was born in Kentucky and possessed all the charm of a Southern belle in addition to the practicality of a pioneer woman.

Lincoln was still working in a store in New Salem when he first met her and proposed to her. She accepted, and they were engaged to be married. However, Lincoln thought he was too poor to support her properly, so he asked her to wait until he could improve his financial condition. During this time he was studying intensively to learn the law.

Before their wedding day arrived, Anne Rutledge was attacked by a sudden and fatal fever. Her death was such a blow to Lincoln that his friends feared for his sanity.

One stormy night two friends found Lincoln standing over her grave. With tears streaming down his face he said, "I cannot bear to let the rain fall on her."

This poem, written by Edgar Lee Masters, is engraved on her tombstone at Petersburg, Illinois:

I am Ann Rutledge who sleep beneath these weeds,
Beloved in life of Abraham Lincoln,
Wedded to him, not through union,
But through separation.
Bloom forever, O Republic,
From the dust of my bosom.

S

SACRIFICE

Dear Madam, I have been shown in the files of the War Department a statement of the Adjutant-General of Massachusetts that you are the mother of five sons who have died gloriously on the field of battle. I feel how weak and fruitless must be any words of mine which should attempt to beguile you from the grief of a loss so overwhelming. But I cannot refrain from tendering to you the consolation that may be found in the thanks of the Republic they died to save. I pray that our heavenly Father may assuage the anguish of your bereavement, and leave you only the cherished memory of the loved and lost, and the solemn pride that must be yours to have laid so costly a sacrifice upon the altar of freedom.

—Letter to Mrs. Bixby, November 21, 1864

SALVATION

The historian John McMaster recalled that as a boy his first sight of Lincoln was at a reception where the guests were ushered past the president and not allowed to come too close. An old man, disappointed at not having shaken hands with the president, waved his hat and called out, "Mr. President, I'm from up in New York State where we believe that God Almighty and Abraham Lincoln are going to save this country."

Hearing this remark, Lincoln smiled and nodded. "My friend," he said, "you're half right."

(see CIVIL WAR, GOD, PRAYER)

SAMENESS

President Lincoln sometimes grew exasperated with Congress for its failure to form enough of a consensus to pass any important new legislation.

"There was a man down in Maine," the president told one of his supporters, "who kept a grocery store, and a lot of fellows used to loaf around for their toddy. He gave them only New England rum, and they drank a pretty considerable quantity of it. But after a while they began to get tired of the stuff and kept asking for something new—something new—all the time. Well, one night, when the whole crowd was gathered around, the grocer brought out his best glasses and says he, 'Well, boys, I've got Something New for you to drink now.'

" 'What is it?' asked the boys, licking their lips in anticipation.

" 'Here you are,' said the grocer, setting out a jug, 'It's New England rum!'

The president paused, then added: "I guess we're a

good deal like the boys, and Congress is a good deal like that grocer.''

(see CONGRESS)

SECESSION

It is an issue which can only be tried by war and decided by victory.

—Message to Congress, 1864
(see ANARCHY)

SELF-DEFENSE

In his biography of Abraham Lincoln, Judge H. W. Beckwith recalled an example of how in court Lincoln the lawyer would condense the facts of a case and the law of the land into a simple little story that any juror could understand.

"A man, by vile words, first provoked and then made bodily attack upon another. The latter, in defending himself, gave the other much the worst of the encounter. The aggressor, to get even, had the one who thrashed him tried in our Circuit Court on a charge of an assault and battery. Mr. Lincoln defended, and told the jury that his client was in the fix of a man who, in going along the highway with a pitchfork on his shoulder, was attacked by a fierce dog that ran out at him from a farmer's door-yard. In parrying off the brute with the fork, its prongs stuck into the brute and killed him.

" 'What made you kill my dog?' said the farmer.

" 'What made him try to bite me?'

" 'But why did you not go at him with the other end of the pitchfork?'

" 'Why did he not come after me with his other end?'

"At this Mr. Lincoln whirled about in his long arms an imaginary dog, and pushed its tail end toward the jury. This was the defensive plea of *'son assault de-mesne'*—loosely, that 'the other fellow brought on the fight,'—quickly told, and in a way that the dullest mind would grasp and retain.''

(see LATIN, PUBLIC SPEAKING)

SELF-GOVERNMENT

The doctrine of self-government is right—absolutely and eternally right.

—Speech, Peoria, Illinois, October 16, 1854

I trust I understand, and truly estimate the right of self-government. My faith in the proposition that each man should do precisely as he pleases with all which is exclusively his own, lies at the foundation of the sense of justice there is in me. I extend the principles to communities of men, as well as to individuals.

—Speech, Peoria, Illinois, October 16, 1854
(see GOVERNMENT, REPUBLICANISM)

SELF-WORTH

It is difficult to make a man miserable while he feels he is worthy of himself and claims kindred to the great God who made him.

—Address to a Negro deputation at Washington, D.C., August 14, 1862

SEX

No matter how much cats fight, there always seem to be plenty of kittens.

—Attributed

SHARING

One time Abraham Lincoln was seen by a neighbor carrying his two sons, Willie and Tad, who were yelling at each other, punching and paddling the air.

"What's wrong?" asked the neighbor.

"Just what's the matter with the whole world," said Lincoln. "I've got three walnuts and each wants two."

(see BOYS)

SHOES

A foreign diplomat was ushered in to see President Lincoln in the White House and found the president busily blacking his shoes.

"Mr. President!" cried the diplomat in amazement. "Do you black your own shoes?"

"Why, yes," shrugged Lincoln. "Whose do you black?"

SKUNKS

Early in his administration, President Lincoln decided to appoint a new secretary of war, and the leading Republicans in the Senate thought it was an opportune time to replace all seven cabinet ministers. Lincoln was advised to make a clean sweep of the cabinet and to select seven new men to bolster the flagging confidence of his countrymen.

The president listened to a group of senators present this argument, then replied with a grin:

"Gentlemen, your request for a change of the whole cabinet because I have made one change reminds me of a story I once heard in Illinois of a farmer who was much

173

troubled by skunks. His wife demanded that he get rid of them.

"The farmer loaded his shotgun one moonlit night and went outside to await bushy-tailed visitors. After some time the wife heard the shotgun go off, and soon afterward the farmer entered the house and wiped his boots.

" 'What luck have you had?' asked the wife.

" 'I hid myself behind the woodpile,' said the farmer, 'with the shotgun pointed toward the hen roost, and before long there appeared not one skunk but seven. I took aim, blazed away, and killed one, and he raised such a fearful smell that I thought it was best, dear, to let the other six go.' "

(see CABINET)

SLANDER

Truth is generally the best vindication against slander.

—Letter to Secretary of War Edwin M. Stanton, July 18, 1864

SLAVERY

Abraham Lincoln's most famous speech on the subject of slavery was delivered at the Republican state convention in Springfield, Illinois, on June 17, 1858. With ominous words that augured the coming of the Civil War he said:

" 'A house divided against itself cannot stand.' I believe this government cannot endure permanently half-slave and half-free. I do not expect the Union to be dissolved—I do not expect the house to fall—but I do expect it will cease to be divided. It will become all one thing, or all the other. Either the opponents of slavery will arrest the further spread of it, and place it where the public mind shall rest in the belief that it is in the course of ultimate extinction; or its advocates will push it forward, till it shall become alike lawful in all the States, old as well as new—North as well as South.''

If slavery is not wrong, nothing is wrong.
—Letter to A. G. Hodges, April 4, 1864

I hate it because of the monstrous injustice of slavery itself. I hate it because it deprives our republican example of its just influence in the world—enables the enemies of free institutions, with plausibility, to taunt us as hypocrites—causes the real friends of freedom to doubt our sincerity and especially because it forces so many really good men amongst ourselves into an open war with the very fundamental principles of civil liberty—criticizing the Declaration of Independence, and insisting there is no right principle of action but *self-interest.*
—Reply to Stephen A. Douglas, October 18, 1854

Whenever I hear anyone arguing for slavery, I feel a strong impulse to see it tried on him personally.
—Address to an Indiana regiment, March 17, 1865

My ancient faith teaches me that ''all men are created equal''; and that there can be no moral right in connection with one man's making a slave of another.
—Speech, Peoria, Illinois, October 16, 1854

In giving freedom to the slave we assure freedom to the free—honorable alike in what we give and what we preserve.
—Second Annual Message to Congress,
December 1, 1862
(see CHARITY, EMANCIPATION, FREEDOM, LABOR,
REPUBLICANISM, RIGHT AND WRONG, TYRANNY)

SLEEP

Men of conscience lose many nights of sleep. Judge Lyle Dickey of Illinois related in his memoirs that when the excitement over the Kansas-Nebraska bill first broke out, he was with Abraham Lincoln attending court. One night several persons, including himself and Lincoln, stayed up late debating the slavery question. Lincoln argued that ultimately slavery would become extinct. Dickey asserted that slavery was an institution that was recognized by the Constitution and that therefore could not be abolished.

"After a while," Dickey recalled, "we went upstairs to bed. There were two beds in our room, and I remember that Lincoln sat up in his nightshirt on the edge of the bed arguing the point with me. At last I drifted off to sleep. Early in the morning I woke up and there was Lincoln sitting up in bed.

" 'Dickey,' said he, 'I tell you this nation cannot exist half slave and half free.'

" 'Oh, Lincoln,' said I, 'go to sleep.' "

SMALLPOX

One day President Lincoln was feeling ill and grew fidgety in the presence of a young man seeking an appointment to the post office.

While the applicant was extolling his own virtues, Lincoln's physician entered the room.

"Doctor, what are these blotches?" asked Lincoln, holding out his hands for the doctor's inspection.

"That's varioloid," said the physician, "a mild smallpox."

"They're all over me," said Lincoln. "Is it contagious?"

"Very contagious," nodded the doctor.

Lincoln's caller leapt to his feet. "Well, I can't stop now, sir. I just wanted to see how you were."

"Oh, don't be in such a hurry," said Lincoln, grinning good-naturedly.

"Thank you, sir," said the visitor. "I'll call again." And in a moment he was out the door.

"There is one good thing about this," Lincoln observed after the man left. "I now have something I can give everybody."

SOLDIER

I am sorry it was not a general—I could make more of them.

—Remark on hearing of the death of a private

I personally wish Jacob Freese, of New Jersey, to be appointed colonel of a colored regiment, and this regardless of whether he can tell the exact shade of Julius Caesar's hair.

—Letter to Secretary of War Edwin M. Stanton, 1863*

We are met on a great battlefield of that war. We have come to dedicate a portion of that field as a final resting place for those who here gave their lives that that nation might live. It is altogether fitting and proper that we should do this. But in a larger sense, we cannot dedicate—we cannot consecrate—we cannot hallow—this ground. The brave men, living and dead, who struggled here, have consecrated it far above our poor power to add or detract. The world will little note nor long re-

*(Lincoln, in a humorous mood, is having some fun with the serious, staid Stanton.)

member what we say here, but it can never forget what they did here.

—Gettysburg Address, November 19, 1863

STANTON, EDWIN M.

President Lincoln received many complaints about the dictatorial style of Secretary of War Edwin M. Stanton but refused to fire him.

"We may have to treat Stanton," said the president, "as they are sometimes obliged to treat a Methodist minister I know out West. He gets wrought up to so high a pitch of excitement in his prayers and exhortations that they have to put bricks in his pockets to keep him down. But I guess we'll let him jump awhile first."

On another occasion an aide told Lincoln that Stanton had called him a damned fool. Other presidents would have considered this remark grounds for dismissal, but Lincoln shrugged it off. "If Stanton said I was a damned fool, then I must be one, for he is nearly always right and generally means what he says."

(see CABINET)

STATESMANSHIP

Honest statesmanship is the wise employment of individual meanness for the public good.

—Attributed

STORYTELLING

It is testimony to Abraham Lincoln's greatness that a man known for his honesty could also be renowned for his storytelling. However, Lincoln's stories were a way of conveying truths, not a way of beautifying lies.

Lincoln once told Chauncey Depew, who was himself a famous raconteur, "They say I tell a great many stories; I reckon I do, but I have found in the course of long experience that common people, take them as they run, are more easily informed through the medium of a broad illustration than in any other way, and as to what the hypocritical few may think, I don't care."

There are even stories about Lincoln's storytelling. The reminiscences of a court clerk reveal Lincoln as an irrepressible storyteller:

"I was never fined but once for contempt of court. Davis fined me five dollars. Mr. Lincoln had just come in, and leaning over my desk had told me a story so irresistibly funny that I broke out into a loud laugh. The judge called me to order, saying, 'This must be stopped. Mr. Lincoln, you are constantly disturbing this court with your stories.' Then to me: 'You may fine yourself five dollars.' I apologized, but told the judge the story was worth the money. In a few minutes the judge called me to him. 'What was that story Lincoln told you?' he asked. I told him, and he laughed aloud in spite of himself. 'Remit your fine,' he ordered."

(see HUMOR)

SUCCESS

The result is not doubtful. We shall not fail—if we stand firm, we shall not fail.

—Speech, to Republican Convention,
Springfield, Illinois, June 16, 1858

SUGAR-COATING

The government printer, whose name was Morris Defrees, was disturbed by the president's use of colloquialisms in his message to Congress. Particularly objectionable to Defrees was the use of the term *sugar-coated*.

"Sir," said Defrees, who was encouraged by Lincoln to speak freely, "a message to Congress is quite another matter from a speech at a mass meeting in Illinois. Your messages to Congress become a part of history and should be written accordingly."

"What is the matter this time?" asked the president.

"In your message you have used an undignified expression." He read aloud the paragraph in which the term *sugar-coated* occurred. "I would alter the structure of that, if I were you."

Lincoln shook his head. "Defrees," he said, "that word expresses precisely my idea, and I am not going to change it. The time will never come in this country when people won't know exactly what *sugar-coated* means."

SWEARING

At a White House reception, General Clinton B. Fisk noticed an old Tennessee farmer waiting in the anteroom and learned that the farmer had been waiting three or four days to get an audience with President Lincoln, hoping to save the life of his son, who had been sentenced to death by a military court.

General Fisk felt sorry for the old man, wrote a brief outline of his case on a card, and sent it in to the president with a special request that Lincoln see the old fellow.

In a few minutes the order came, and the farmer was trotted past impatient governors, congressmen, and generals. He presented some papers to President Lincoln, who promised to look into the case and give him an answer the next day.

The old man looked into Lincoln's care-worn face and

cried: "But tomorrow may be too late! My son is under sentence of death!"

Lincoln saw the tears streaming down the old man's face and said, soothingly, "Let me tell you a story about General Fisk, the man who asked me to see you. The general began his military life as a colonel, and when he raised his regiment in Missouri he told them that to maintain discipline, he would do all the swearing of the regiment. The men promised to abide by this rule, and for some months no one violated that promise.

"The colonel had a teamster in his regiment named John Todd, who, as roads were in poor repair out there, had some difficulty in commanding his temper and taming his tongue. One day John happened to be driving a mule team through a series of mudholes a little worse than usual, when, unable to restrain himself any longer, he burst forth into a volley of energetic oaths.

"The colonel heard of the offense and brought John to account.

" 'John,' said he, 'didn't you promise to let me do all the swearing of the regiment?'

" 'Yes, I did, Colonel,'' he answered, 'but the fact was, the swearing had to be done then or not at all, and you weren't there to do it.' "

The old man laughed, forgetting for a moment about his griefs and his cares, and Lincoln laughed with him. Then the president wrote a few words on a slip of paper and handed it to the old man. Once again tears streamed down the old farmer's face, but this time they were tears of joy, for the words saved the life of his son.

(see HANDSOME, PARDON, REPRIEVE)

TACT

Tact is the ability to describe others as they see themselves.

—Attributed

TASTE

Social reformer Robert Dale Owen, author of a book on spiritualism, once cornered President Lincoln at a private party and, finding him open-minded about spiritual matters, insisted on reading to him a long manuscript on the subject of spiritualism. Lincoln listened quietly and then, when Owen asked his opinion of the booklet, replied, ''Well, for those who like that sort of thing I should think that is just about the sort of thing they would like.''

TERRITORY

A nation may be said to consist of its territory, its people, and its laws. The territory is the only part which is of certain durability.

—Second Annual Message to Congress,
December 1, 1862

TESTIMONY

During the Civil War rumors circulated around Washington that there was a spy in the White House who was a woman. The Senate Committee on the Conduct of the War scheduled a secret meeting to discuss reports that Mrs. Lincoln, whose nervous behavior was often baffling, was the traitor in question.

A member of the committee recorded what transpired: "We had just been called to order by the chairman when, at the foot of the committee table, his hat in hand, his form towering, was Abraham Lincoln. No one spoke, for no one knew what to say. At last the caller spoke slowly, with control, though with a depth of sorrow in the tone of his voice: 'I, Abraham Lincoln, president of the United States, appear of my own volition before this committee to say that I, of my own knowledge, know it is untrue that any member of my family holds treasonable communication with the enemy.'

"Having attested this, he went away as silent and solitary as he had come. We sat for some minutes speechless. Then, by tacit agreement, no word being spoken, the committee dropped all considerations of the rumors that the wife of the president was betraying the Union."

THANKSGIVING

In October 1863, although the nation was rent by the Civil War and his heart was wrung by the death and suffering inflicted upon so many people on both sides of the conflict, Lincoln still found much for which to be thankful.

He issued a Thanksgiving Day Proclamation that established an American tradition that is still observed today:

"The year that is drawing to its close has been filled with the blessings of fruitful fields and healthful skies. To these bounties, which are so constantly enjoyed that we are prone to forget the source from which they come, others have been added which are of so extraordinary a nature that they cannot fail to penetrate and soften the heart which is habitually insensible to the ever watchful providence of Almighty God. . . .

"Needful diversions of wealth and strength from the fields of peaceful industry to the national defense have not arrested the plow, the shuttle, or the ship. . . . Population has steadily increased . . . and the country, rejoicing in the consciousness of augmented strength and vigor, is permitted to expect continuance of years with large increase of freedom.

"No human counsel hath devised, nor hath any mortal hand worked out these great things. They are the gracious gifts of the Most High God, who, while dealing with us in anger for our sins, hath nevertheless remembered mercy.

"It has seemed to me fit and proper that they should be solemnly, reverently, and gratefully acknowledged as with one heart and one voice by the whole American people. I do therefore invite my fellow citizens in every part of the United States, and also those who are at sea and those who are sojourning in foreign lands, to set apart and observe the last Thursday of November next, as a day of Thanksgiving and Praise to our beneficent Father who dwelleth in the Heavens. . . ."

On November 28, 1863, the nation officially observed the first Thanksgiving Day. According to Lincoln's proclamation, it was to be the fourth Thursday in November. In 1941 Congress changed it to the third Thursday, where it now stands as a distinctly American holiday.

(see PRAYER)

TIME

On the pages of the one notebook that remains as a record of Lincoln's brief career as a schoolboy are found some lines of a poem believed to be original with him:

Time, what an empty vapor 'tis,
    And days, how swift they are;
Swift as an Indian arrow—
    Fly on like a shooting star.

The present moment just is here,
    Then slides away in haste,
That we can never say they're ours,
    But only say they're past.

Time is everything. Please act in view of this.

—Letter to Union governors, July 3, 1862

TITLES

Abraham Lincoln, like many Americans raised on the frontier, was unimpressed by titles. Once an Austrian count applied for a position in the Union army, stressing his family honor and ancestry and repeatedly reminding the president that he held the high title of count.

Taking his application, Lincoln patted the man on the shoulder sympathetically and said, "Never mind, don't you worry, you shall be treated with just as much consideration. I will see to it that your bearing a title shan't be held against you."

(see ANCESTORS, DAVIS)

TRUST

If you once forfeit the confidence of your fellow citizens, you can never regain their respect and esteem.

—McClure, *Lincoln's Yarns and Stories*, 1904

TRUTH

I am a firm believer in the people. If given the truth, they can be depended upon to meet any national crisis. The great point is to bring them the real facts.

—Attributed

TWO-FACED

During a debate, Stephen A. Douglas accused Abraham Lincoln of being two-faced.

"I leave it to you, my friends," Lincoln retorted, turning toward his audience. "If I had two faces, would I be wearing this one?"

(see DEBATE, HOMELINESS)

TYRANNY

Familiarize yourselves with the chains of bondage and you prepare your own limbs to wear them. Accustomed to trample on the rights of others, you have lost the genius of your own independence and become the fit subjects of the first cunning tyrant who rises among you.

—Speech at Edwardsville, Illinois, September 11, 1858
(see REPUBLICANISM, SLAVERY)

UNION

If we do not make common cause to save the good old ship of the Union on this voyage, nobody will have a chance to pilot her on another voyage.

—Address at Cleveland, Ohio, February 15, 1861

I therefore consider that, in view of the Constitution and the laws, the Union is unbroken.

—First Inaugural Address, March 4, 1861

Continue to execute all the express provisions of our national Constitution, and the Union will endure forever.

—First Inaugural Address, March 4, 1861
(see CIVIL WAR, SECESSION)

V

VICE-PRESIDENT

On November 6, 1860, Abraham Lincoln was elected president of the United States. On November 8, he wrote a letter to his running mate Hannibal Hamlin, the Republican party's winning vice-presidential candidate, saying, "I am anxious for a personal interview with you."

The two men had run together on the same winning Republican ticket, but had not yet met.

VICES

Abraham Lincoln enjoyed relating an experience he had one time riding in a stage coach with an old Kentucky gentleman. The old gentleman was surprised when Lincoln turned down offers of both tobacco and brandy.

When their journey together was at an end, the Kentuckian shook hands with Lincoln and said, "See here, young man, you're a clever but strange companion. I may never see you again, and I don't want to offend you, but I want to say this: My experience has taught me that folks who have no vices have very few virtues.''

VICTORY

Wise councils may accelerate or mistakes delay it, but sooner or later the victory is sure to come.

—Speech, Springfield, Illinois, June 16, 1858

VIOLENCE

Among free men there can be no successful appeal from the ballot to the bullet, and . . . they who take such appeal are sure to lose their case and pay the cost.

—Letter to James. C. Conkling, August 26, 1863
(see ELECTIONS, VOTE)

VOTE

The ballot is stronger than the bullet.

—Speech at Bloomington, Illinois, May 19, 1856
(see ELECTIONS, VOTE)

WASHINGTON, GEORGE

Washington is the mightiest name of the earth—long since mightiest in the cause of civil liberty, still mightiest in moral reformation. On that name no eulogy is expected. It cannot be. To add brightness to the sun or glory to the name of Washington is alike impossible. Let none attempt it. In solemn awe pronounce the name, and in its naked deathless splendor leave it shining on.

—Address, Springfield, Illinois, February 22, 1842
(see BOOKS)

WEDDING

The greatest social event in many a year in Spencer, Indiana, was the wedding of Reuben and Charles Grigsby to Elizabeth Ray and Matilda Hawkins, respectively, in a double wedding held at the home of the senior Reuben Grigsby.

Most of the county was invited, but the Lincolns were

omitted. Feeling slighted, Abraham wrought a satirical revenge by writing what he called "The Chronicles of Reuben." Eventually published in the newspapers, Lincoln's manuscript was lost for many years until it was found at the home of Redmond Grigsby in Rockport, Indiana.

The Chronicles of Reuben

Now, there was a man whose name was Reuben, and the same was very great in substance, in horses and cattle and swine, and a very great household.

It came to pass when the sons of Reuben grew up that they were desirous of taking to themselves wives, and, being too well known as to honor in their own country, they took a journey into a far country and there procured for themselves wives.

It came to pass also that when they were about to make the return home they sent a messenger before them to bear the tidings to their parents.

These, inquiring of the messenger what time their sons and wives would come, made a great feast and called all their kinsmen and neighbors in, and made great preparation.

When the time drew nigh, they sent out two men to meet the grooms and their brides, with a trumpet to welcome them, and to accompany them.

When they came near unto the house of Reuben, the father, the messenger came before them and gave a shout, and the whole multitude ran out with shouts of joy and music, playing on all kinds of instruments.

Some were playing on harps, some on violins, and some blowing on rams' horns.

Some also were casting dust and ashes toward Heaven, and chief among them all was Josiah, blowing his bugle and making sounds so great the neighboring hills and valleys echoed with the resounding acclamation.

When they had played and their harps had sounded till the grooms and brides approached the gates, Reuben, the father, met them and welcomed them to his house.

The wedding feast being now ready, they were all invited to sit down and eat, placing the bridegrooms and their brides at each end of the table.

Waiters were then appointed to serve and wait on the guests. When all had eaten and were full and merry, they went out again and played and sung till night.

And when they had made an end of feasting and rejoicing the multitude dispersed, each going to his own home.

The family then took seats with their waiters to converse while preparations were being made in two upper chambers for the brides and grooms.

This being done, the waiters took the two brides upstairs, placing one in a room at the right hand of the stairs and the other on the left.

The waiters came down, and Nancy, the mother, then gave directions to the waiters of the bridegrooms, and they took them upstairs, but placed them in the wrong rooms.

The waiters then all came downstairs.

But the mother, being fearful of a mistake, made inquiry of the waiters, and learning the true facts, took the light and sprang upstairs.

It came to pass she ran to one of the rooms and exclaimed, "O Lord, Reuben, you are with the wrong wife."

The young men, both alarmed at this, ran out with such violence against each other, they came near knocking each other down.

The tumult gave evidence to those below that the mistake was certain.

At last they all came down and had a long conversation about who made the mistake, but it could not be decided.

So ended the chapter.

"Yes, they did have a joke on us," recalled Elizabeth Grigsby, when a reporter asked her about Lincoln's outrageous story. "They said my man got into the wrong room and Charles got into my room. But it wasn't so.

Lincoln just wrote that for mischief. Abe and my man often laughed about that."

(see HUMOR, JOKING)

WEIGHTY MEN

A Delaware congressman brought a group of prominent citizens from Wilmington to see President Lincoln, introducing them with the comment: "Mr. President, these are among the weightiest men in Delaware."

"So you are the weighty men of Delaware?" asked the president with a twinkle in his eye. "All from New Castle County? Did it ever occur to you gentlemen there was danger that your little state might tip up during your absence?"

WHIGS

Before he was a Republican, Abraham Lincoln was a Whig. During one of the debates with Stephen A. Douglas, Lincoln said in reply to his adversary: "Fellow-citizens, my friend, Mr. Douglas, made the startling announcement today that the Whigs are all dead. If that be so, fellow-citizens, you will now experience the novelty of hearing a speech from a dead man, and I suppose you might properly say, in the language of the old hymn, 'Hark! from the tombs a doleful sound!' "

(see DEBATE, TWO-FACED)

WORDS

He can compress the most words into the smallest ideas of any man I ever met.

—Gross, *Lincoln's Own Stories*, p. 36
(of a fellow lawyer)
(see BREVITY, EXPLANATIONS)

WORK

My father taught me to work, but not to love it. I never did like to work, and I don't deny it. I'd rather read, tell stories, crack jokes, talk, laugh—anything but work.

—Attributed
(see HUMOR)

WORKERS

The strongest bond of human sympathy outside the family relation should be one uniting all working people of all nations and tongues, and kindreds. Nor should this lead us to a war on property, or the owners of property. Property is the fruit of labor; property is desirable; is a positive good in the world. That some should be rich shows that others may become rich and, hence, is just encouragement to industry and enterprise.

—Reply to New York Workingmen's Association,
March 21, 1864
(see ENTERPRISE, LABOR, PROPERTY)

WRITING

The precise period at which writing was invented is not known, but it certainly was as early as the time of Moses; from which we may safely infer that its inventors were very Old Fogies.

—Lecture, Jacksonville, Illinois, February 11, 1859

Selections from

A BRIEF BIOGRAPHY
OF ABRAHAM LINCOLN

*The Most Important Events
and Words in Lincoln's Life*

~ 1809 ~

Abraham Lincoln is born in a log cabin near Hodgenville in what is now Larue County, Kentucky. His family is poor, but his ancestors are not without distinction. Genealogical research will later reveal that he is descended from the Revolutionary War General Benjamin Lincoln, who took the sword from British General Cornwallis at Yorktown. Other Lincoln ancestors include two early governors of Massachusetts and a governor of Maine.

I was born, February 22, 1809, in Hardin County, Kentucky. My parents were both born in Virginia, of undistinguished families—second families, perhaps I should say. My mother, who died in my tenth year, was of a family of the name of Hanks, some of whom now reside in Adams and others in Macon County, Illinois.

My paternal grandfather, Abraham Lincoln, emigrated from Rockingham County, Virginia, to Kentucky, about 1781 or 1782, where, a year or two later, he was killed by Indians, not in battle, but by stealth, when he was laboring to open a farm in the forest. His ancestors, who were Quakers, went to Virginia from Berks County, Pennsylvania. An effort to identify them with the New England family of the same name ended in nothing more than a similarity of Christian names in both families, such as Enoch, Levi, Mordecai, Solomon, Abraham, and the like.

—Letter to Jesse W. Fell, December 20, 1859

~ 1816–18 ~

The Lincoln family moves to Indiana when Abe is eight. His mother, Nancy Hanks Lincoln (1784–1818), dies two years later, and his father marries Sarah Bush Johnson (1788–1869), a widow with three children. Lincoln's early schooling is deficient, but he supplements it with reading on his own.

My father, at the death of his father, was but six years of age, and he grew up literally without education. He removed from Kentucky to what is now Spencer County, Indiana, in my eighth year. We reached our new home about the time the State came into the Union (1816).

It was a wild region, with many bears and other wild animals still in the woods. There I grew up. There were some schools, so-called, but no qualification was ever required of a teacher beyond readin,' writin,' and cipherin' to the Rule of Three. If a straggler, supposed to understand Latin, happened to sojourn in the neighborhood, he was looked upon as a wizard.

There was absolutely nothing to excite ambition for education. Of course, when I came of age, I did not know much. Still, somehow, I could read, write, and cipher to the Rule of Three, but that was all. I have not been to school since. The little advance I now have upon this store of education I have picked up from time to time under the pressure of necessity.

—Letter to Jesse W. Fell, December 20, 1859

~ 1816–30 ~

Later in life, at the age of thirty-five, Abraham Lincoln will return to visit his old home in Indiana, and though he has described the place "as unpoetical as any spot on earth," he is moved to write a poem about it.

My childhood-home I see again,
    And gladden with the view;
And still as mem'ries crowd my brain,
    There's sadness in it, too.

O memory! thou mid-way world
    'Twixt Earth and Paradise,
Where things decayed, and loved ones lost
    In dreamy shadows rise. . . .

I range the fields with pensive tread,
    And pace the hollow rooms;
And feel (companions of the dead)
    I'm living in the tombs. . . .

Now fare thee well: more thou the cause
    Than subject now of woe.
All mental pangs, but time's kind laws,
    Hast lost the power to know.

And now away to seek some scene
    Less painful than the last—
With less of horror mingled in
    The present and the past.

The very spot where grew the bread
    That formed my bones, I see.

How strange, old field, on thee to tread,
And feel I'm part of thee!

—My Childhood Home I See Again, 1844

~ 1827 ~

*A fledgling writer, young Abraham Lincoln composes poems
and essays. His first published piece is an essay on "National
Politics," printed in a small newspaper when Lincoln is eigh-
teen years old.*

The American government is the best form of government for an intelligent people. It ought to be kept sound,
and preserved forever, that general education should be
fostered and carried all over the country; that the Constitution should be saved, the Union perpetuated and
the laws revered, respected and enforced.

—"National Politics," essay, 1827

~ 1829 ~

*By the time he is nineteen, Abraham Lincoln is six feet four
inches tall, a towering figure who commands attention wherever he goes. He is destined to be the tallest of all the American
presidents, one and a half inches taller than Thomas Jefferson
and two inches taller than George Washington.*

If any personal description of me is thought desirable,
it may be said, I am, in height, six feet four inches,
nearly; lean in flesh, weighing, on an average, one hundred and eighty pounds; dark complexion, with coarse

black hair, and gray eyes. No other marks or brands recollected.

—Letter to Jesse W. Fell, December 20, 1859

~ 1830 ~

In March 1830, Abe Lincoln moves with his father's family to Illinois, the state with which his name will eternally be linked, settling in New Salem near Springfield. Abe continues farming until 1831, when at the age of twenty-two, he seeks other forms of employment for his talents.

I was raised to farm-work, which I continued until I was twenty-two. At twenty-one I came into Illinois and passed the first year in Macon County. Then I got to New Salem, at that time in Sangamo, now in Menard County, where I remained a year as a sort of clerk in a store.

—Letter to Jesse W. Fell, December 20, 1859

~ 1830–32 ~

Abe Lincoln leaves the farm at age twenty-two and works at a variety of jobs before serving briefly as a captain in the Black Hawk Indian War, where he sees no combat. Captain Lincoln is disciplined several times for unmilitary conduct. He breaks a rule by firing a gun "within the limits" and has his sword taken from him. On another occasion, some of his men steal some liquor, get drunk, and become unfit for duty. As the responsible officer, Lincoln is condemned to wear a wooden sword for two days. However, it is his first taste of leadership, and he is exhilarated by it. Returning to civilian life after three months, he runs for the Illinois legislature and loses.

Then came the Black Hawk War, and I was elected a captain of volunteers—a success which gave me more pleasure than any I have had since. I went through the campaign, was elated, ran for the Legislature in the same year (1832), and was beaten—the only time I have ever been beaten by the people.

—Letter to Jesse W. Fell, December 20, 1859

~ 1832 ~

On March 9, 1832, Abraham Lincoln throws his hat into the political ring for the first time, announcing his candidacy for the Illinois State Assembly. Only twenty-three, young Lincoln loses the election, but his eloquence, exhibited by this announcement, does not pass wholly unnoticed.

Every man is said to have his peculiar ambition. Whether it be true or not, I can say for one that I have no other so great as that of being truly esteemed by my fellow men, by rendering myself worthy of their esteem. How far I shall succeed in gratifying this ambition, is yet to be developed.

I am young and unknown to many of you. I was born and have ever remained in the most humble walks of life. I have no wealthy or popular relations to recommend me. My case is thrown exclusively upon the independent voters of this county, and if elected they will have conferred a favor upon me, for which I shall be unremitting in my labors to compensate. But if the good people in their wisdom shall see fit to keep me in the background, I have been too familiar with disappointments to be very much chagrined.

—Communication to the people of Sangamo County, Illinois (March 9, 1832)

~ 1834–40 ~

Lincoln runs for the legislature again with more success in 1834, and with his gregarious, easygoing nature and his droll sense of humor, he becomes a popular leader of the Illinois frontier community.

The next, and three succeeding biennial elections, I was elected to the Legislature. I was not a candidate afterwards. During this legislative period, I had studied law and removed to Springfield to practice it.

—Letter to Jesse W. Fell, December 20, 1859

~ 1835–36 ~

His legislative work brings him into contact with other lawyers, and he decides to study law himself. Reading law books alone in New Salem, Abraham Lincoln is able to pass the bar in 1836.

If you are resolutely determined to make a lawyer of yourself, the thing is more than half done already. It is but a small matter whether you read *with* anybody or not. I did not read with anyone. Get the books, and read and study them till you understand them in their principal features; and that is the main thing. It is of no consequence to be in a large town while you are reading. I read at New Salem, which never had 300 people living in it. The *books*, and your *capacity* for understanding them, are just the same in all places.

—Letter to Isham Reavis, November 5, 1855

~ 1836–37 ~

Abraham Lincoln's engagement to Anne Rutledge of New Salem, his first love, is ended by her death from a sudden illness. Searching for another mate, Lincoln courts Mary Owens, but the romance is an ambivalent one that is never consummated in marriage. Lincoln's account of this sad affair illustrates his character more than his common sense.

Without apologizing for being egotistical, I shall make the history of so much of my own life, as has elapsed since I saw you, the subject of this letter. . . .

It was . . . in the autumn of 1836, that a married lady of my acquaintance, and who was a great friend of mine, being about to pay a visit to her father and other relatives residing in Kentucky, proposed to me, that on her return she would bring a sister of hers with her, upon condition that I would engage to become her brother-in-law with all convenient dispatch. I, of course, accepted the proposal; for you know I could not have done otherwise, had I really been averse to it; but privately between you and me, I was most confoundedly well pleased with the project. I had seen the said sister some three years before, thought her intelligent and agreeable, and saw no good objection to plodding life through hand in hand with her. Time passed on, the lady took her journey and in due time returned, sister in company sure enough. . . .

In a few days we had an interview, and although I

had seen her before, she did not look as my imagination had pictured her. I knew she was over-size, but she now appeared a fair match for Falstaff; I knew she was called an "old maid," and I felt no doubt of the truth of at least half of the appellation; but now, when I beheld her, I could not for my life avoid thinking of my mother; and this, not from withered features, for her skin was too full of fat, to permit its contracting into wrinkles; but from her want of teeth, weather-beaten appearance in general, and from a kind of notion that ran into my head, that nothing could have commenced at the size of infancy, and reached her present bulk in less than thirty-five or forty years; and, in short, I was not all pleased with her.

But what could I do? I had told her sister that I would take her for better or for worse; and I made it a point of honor and conscience in all things, to stick to my word, especially if others had been induced to act on it, which in this case, I doubted not they had, for I was now fairly convinced that no other man on earth would have her, and hence the conclusion that they were bent on holding me to my bargain.

Well, thought I, I have said, and be consequences what they may, it shall not be my fault if I fail to do it. At once I determined to consider her my wife; and this done, all my powers of discovery were put to the rack, in search of perfections in her, which might be fairly set-off against her defects. I tried to imagine she was handsome, which, but for unfortunate corpulency, was actually true. Exclusive of this, no woman that I have seen has a finer face. I also tried to convince myself, that the mind was much more to be valued than the person; and in this, she was not inferior, as I could discover, to any with whom I had been acquainted.

Shortly after this, without attempting to come to any positive understanding with her, I set out for Vandalia, where and when you first saw me. During my stay there, I had letters from her, which did not change my opinion of either her intellect or intention; but on the contrary, confirmed it in both. . . .

After my return home, I saw nothing to change my opinion of her in any particular. She was the same and so was I. . . .

After I had delayed the matter as long as I thought I could in honor do, which by the way had brought me round into the last fall, I concluded I might as well bring it to a consummation without further delay; and so I mustered my resolution, and made the proposal to her direct; but, shocking to relate, she answered, No. At first I supposed she did it through an affection of modesty, which I thought but ill-become her, under the peculiar circumstances of her case; but on my renewal of the charge, I found she repelled it with greater firmness than before. I tried it again and again, but with the same success, or rather with the same want of success.

I was finally forced to give it up, at which I very unexpectedly found myself mortified almost beyond endurance. I was mortified, it seemed to me, in a hundred different ways. My vanity was deeply wounded by the reflection, that I had so long been too stupid to discover her intentions, and at the same time never doubting that I understood them perfectly; and lo, that she whom I had taught myself to believe no body else would have, had actually rejected me with all my fancied greatness; and to cap the whole, I then, for the first time, began to suspect that I was really a little in love with her.

—Letter to Mrs. Orville Browning, April 1, 1838

~ 1838 ~

Mary Owens, asked why she refused Lincoln's proposal of marriage, offers this answer: "Mr. Lincoln was deficient in those little links which make up the path of a woman's happiness." The rejected lover vows never to marry—a rare vow that Honest Abe will not keep.

But let it all go. I'll try and out live it. Others have been made fools of by the girls; but this can never be with truth said of me. I most emphatically, in this instance, made a fool of myself. I have now come to the conclusion never again to think of marrying; and for this reason; I can never be satisfied with any one who would be block-head enough to have me.

—Letter to Mrs. Orville Browning, April 1, 1838

~ 1842 ~

Abraham Lincoln falls in love with Mary Todd, the ambitious but unstable daughter of a prominent Springfield family that can trace their ancestry back to the sixth century. "The Todd family are mighty high-class people," Abe muses in Robert Sherwood's play Abe Lincoln in Illinois. *"They spell their name with two D's. Which is mighty impressive, considering one was enough for God." Mary Todd is also courted by Stephen Douglas, Lincoln's rival in love as well as politics. But Mary Todd prefers the lanky Lincoln and marries him on November 4, 1842.*

Abraham Lincoln and Mary Todd, married, November 4, 1842
Robert Todd Lincoln, born, August 1, 1843
Edward B. Lincoln, born, March 10, 1846
William Wallace Lincoln, born, December 21, 1850

Thomas Lincoln, born, April 4, 1853.
Edward B. Lincoln, died, February 1, 1850

—Family record inscribed in Abraham Lincoln's Bible

~ 1843–46 ~

Nine months after the wedding their first child is born, Robert Todd Lincoln. He is the only one of their four sons who will grow to maturity. Although Abraham Lincoln does not run for office again until 1846, he is frequently separated from his wife by his law business.

In this troublesome world we are never quite satisfied. When you were here, I thought you hindered me in attending to business, but now, having nothing but business—no variety—it has grown exceedingly tasteless to me. I hate to sit down and direct documents and I hate to stay in the old room by myself. . . . And you are entirely free from headache? That is good—good—considering it is the first spring you have been free from it since we were acquainted. I am afraid you will get so well, and fat, and young, as to be wanting to marry again.

—Letter to Mary Todd Lincoln, April 16, 1848

~ 1846–54 ~

In 1846, Lincoln is elected to his first and only national office prior to the presidency, a seat in the House of Representatives. In Congress his adamant opposition to the Mexican War costs him much of his popularity, though it earns him some respect among his colleagues for his moral courage. Lincoln does not run for Congress again, and probably would not have won reelection if he had.

In 1846 I was once elected to the lower House of Congress, but was not a candidate for re-election. From 1849 to 1854, both inclusive, practiced law more assiduously than ever before. Always a Whig in politics, and generally on the Whig electoral ticket making canvasses. I was losing interest in politics when the repeal of the Missouri Compromise aroused me again. What I have done since then is pretty well known.

—Letter to Jesse W. Fell, December 20, 1859

~ 1857–58 ~

When the new Republican party is formed, Abraham Lincoln emerges as one of its leaders. In 1858 he is nominated by the Republicans to run against Stephen A. Douglas for the Illinois Senate seat. Accepting the nomination, Lincoln makes one of his greatest speeches, crystallizing the conflict in the national soul.

"A house divided against itself cannot stand." I believe this government cannot endure permanently half slave and half free. I do not expect the Union to be dissolved—I do not expect the house to fall—but I do expect it will cease to be divided. It will become all one thing, or all the other. Either the opponents of slavery will arrest the further spread of it, and place it where the public mind shall rest in the belief that it is in the course of ultimate extinction; or its advocates will push it forward till it shall become alike lawful in all the states, old as well as new, North as well as South.

—Speech at the Republican convention, June 16, 1858

~ 1858 ~

Lincoln challenges Senator Stephen A. Douglas to a series of debates. The better-known Douglas accepts the challenge, and seven debates are held in front of crowds averaging fifteen thousand. Both men gain political stature as a result of these debates, which attract national attention. Although Lincoln loses the senatorial contest, both men become contenders for the presidency in 1860, and both are ultimately nominated by their parties.

Judge Douglas declares that if any community want slavery they have a right to have it. He can say that logically, if he says that there is no wrong in slavery; but if you admit that there is a wrong in it, he cannot logically say that anybody has a right to do wrong.

—Fifth Debate, Galesburg, Illinois, October 7, 1858

~ 1860–61 ~

Abraham Lincoln is elected president with 55.8 percent of the nation's popular vote and 180 electoral votes out of 303, but receives not a single electoral vote from the ten Southern states. He bids farewell to his friends and supporters in Springfield before departing for Washington, amid a flurry of death threats, to assume the duties of the presidency in the midst of the gravest crisis in the history of the United States.

No one, not in my situation, can appreciate my feeling of sadness at this parting. To this place, and the kindness of these people, I owe everything. Here I have lived a quarter of a century, and have passed from a young to an old man. Here my children have been born, and one is buried. I now leave, not knowing when or whether ever I may return, with a task before me greater than that which rested upon Washington. Without the assistance of that Divine Being who ever attended him, I cannot succeed. With that assistance I cannot fail. Trusting in Him who can go with me, and remain with you, and be everywhere for good, let us confidently hope that all will yet be well.

—Farewell Address, Springfield, Illinois,
February 11, 1861

~ 1862 ~

In his Second Annual Message to Congress, Abraham Lincoln justifies the Emancipation Proclamation, which will be issued thirty days later, on January 1, 1863. For Lincoln, the Emancipation Proclamation was nothing less than an act of national salvation.

The dogmas of the quiet past are inadequate to the stormy present. The occasion is piled high with difficulty, and we must rise with the occasion. As our case is new, so we must think anew and act anew. We must disenthrall ourselves, and then we shall save our country.

Fellow citizens, we cannot escape history. We of this Congress and this administration will be remembered in spite of ourselves. No personal significance or insignificance will spare one or another of us. The fiery trial through which we pass will light us down in honor or dishonor to the last generation.

We say we are for the Union. The world will not forget that we say this. We know how to save the Union. The world knows we do know how to save it. We, even we here, hold the power and bear the responsibility. In giving freedom to the slave, we assure freedom to the free—honorable alike in what we give and what we preserve. We shall nobly save or meanly lose the last, best hope of earth. Other means may succeed; this could not fail. The way is plain, peaceful, generous—a way which if followed the world will forever applaud and God must forever bless.

—Second Annual Message to Congress,
December 1, 1862

~ 1863 ~

On November 19, 1863, at the battlefield of Gettysburg, Pennsylvania, Abraham Lincoln delivers a speech that lasts scarcely two minutes, but that will take its place with the Declaration of Independence, the Constitution, and the Bill of Rights as one of the essential documents of the American nation. The Gettysburg Address is not merely a political statement—it is a prophetic expression of the American soul, voiced by an American prophet.

Four score and seven years ago our fathers brought forth on this continent, a new nation, conceived in liberty, and dedicated to the proposition that all men are created equal.

Now we are engaged in a great civil war, testing whether that nation or any nation so conceived and so dedicated can long endure. We are met on a great battlefield of that war. We have come to dedicate a portion of that field, as a final resting-place for those who here gave their lives that that nation might live. It is altogether fitting and proper that we should do this.

But, in a larger sense, we cannot dedicate—we cannot consecrate—we cannot hallow—this ground. The brave men, living and dead, who struggled here, have consecrated it far above our poor power to add or detract. The world will little note, nor long remember, what we say here, but it can never forget what they did here. It is for us, the living, rather to be dedicated here to the unfinished work which they who fought here have thus far so nobly advanced. It is rather for us to be here dedicated to the great task remaining before us—that from these honored dead we take increased devotion to that cause for which they gave the last full measure of devotion; that we here highly resolve that these dead shall not have died in vain; that this nation, under God, shall have a new birth of freedom; and that government of the people, by the people, for the people, shall not perish from the earth.

~ 1864 ~

Receiving the endorsement of the National Union League for his reelection, President Lincoln expresses his desire for reelection with a humility that inspires instinctive trust.

I do not allow myself to suppose that either the convention or the League have concluded to decide that I am either the greatest or best man in America, but rather they have concluded that it is not best to swap horses while crossing the river, and have further concluded that

I am not so poor a horse that they might not make a botch of it in trying to swap.

—Reply to the National Union League, June 9, 1864

~ 1865 ~

In his Second Inaugural Address, President Lincoln calls for an end to the Civil War and a new national unity. The concluding passage is an eloquent moral appeal to the national conscience. These words are now inscribed on the Lincoln Memorial in Washington, D.C.

With malice toward none, with charity for all, with firmness in the right as God gives us to see the right, let us strive on to finish the work we are in, to bind up the nation's wounds, to care for him who shall have borne the battle and for his widow and his orphan, to do all which may achieve and cherish a just and lasting peace among ourselves and with all nations.

—Second Inaugural Address, March 4, 1865

On the night of the surrender of General Robert E. Lee at Appomattox, Lincoln spoke to a joyous crowd outside the White House. Afterward a band played patriotic tunes and the president made a special request.

Play "Dixie" now. It's ours.

—President Lincoln to the bandleader
April 10, 1865

In his final public address, three days before his assassination, President Lincoln looks beyond the Civil War to the problems of Reconstruction.

We meet this evening, not in sorrow, but in gladness of heart. The evacuation of Petersburg and Richmond, and the surrender of the principal insurgent army, give hope of a righteous and speedy peace whose joyous expression can not be restrained. In the midst of this, however, He from Whom all blessings flow, must not be forgotten. A call for a national thanksgiving is being prepared, and will be duly promulgated. Nor must those whose harder part gives us the cause for rejoicing, be overlooked. Their honors must not be parcelled out with others. I myself was near the front, and had the high pleasure of transmitting much of the good news to you, but no part of the honor, for plan or execution, is mine. To General Grant, his skillful officers, and brave men, all belongs. The gallant Navy stood ready, but was not in reach to take active part.

By these recent successes the re-inauguration of the national authority—reconstruction—which has had a large share of thought from the first, is pressed much more closely upon our attention. It is fraught with great difficulty. Unlike the case of a war between independent nations, there is no authorized organ for us to treat with. No one man has authority to give up the rebellion for any other man. We simply must begin with, and mould from, disorganized and discordant elements. Nor is it a small additional embarrassment that we, the loyal people, differ among ourselves as to the mode, manner and means of reconstruction. . . .

Let us all join in doing the acts necessary to restoring the practical relations between these States and the Union, and each forever after innocently indulge his own opinion whether, in doing the acts, he brought the States from without into the Union, or only gave them proper assistance, they never having been out of it.

—Last public address, April 11, 1865

Lincoln's assassination on April 14, 1865, is a tragic loss to the nation and the world, yet it only binds Lincoln more deeply to the common heart and soul of humanity. He is the quintessential American hero, and his martyrdom is the hero's final apotheosis. There are tributes from all over the world to pay him homage, including this one from the pen of the poet Robert Whitaker.

> There is no name in all our country's story
> So loved as his today:
> No name which so unites the things of glory
> With life's plain, common way.

BIBLIOGRAPHY

Anderson, Dwight G. *Abraham Lincoln: The Quest for Immortality.* Alfred A. Knopf, 1982.

Angle, Paul M. *The Lincoln Reader.* Rutgers Univ. Press, 1947.

Angle, Paul and Miers, Earl Schenck, eds. *The Living Lincoln.* Rutgers Univ. Press, 1955.

Appleman, Roy Edgar, ed. *Abraham Lincoln: From His Own Words and Contemporary Accounts.* U.S. National Park Service, 1942.

Barton, William Eleazar. *The Life of Abraham Lincoln* (2 vols.). Bobbs-Merrill, 1925.

Barton, William Eleazar. *Lincoln at Gettysburg.* Bobbs-Merrill, 1930.

Basler, Roy P., ed., and Pratt, Marion Dolores and Dunlap, Lloyd A., asst. ed. *The Collected Works of Abraham Lincoln* (8 vols.). Abraham Lincoln Association, 1953.

Bishop, Jim. *The Day Lincoln Was Shot.* Harper & Brothers, 1955.

Botkin, B.A., ed. *A Treasury of American Folklore.* Crown, 1944.

Brooks, Noah. *Writings of Abraham Lincoln* (edited by A.B. Lapsley). Includes "The Life of Lincoln" by Noah Brooks. Collier, 1905–06.

———*Mr. Lincoln's Washington* (edited by Philip Staudenraus). Yoseloff, 1967.

Carnegie, Dale. *Lincoln, the Unknown.* Appleton, 1932.

Chittenden, L.E., ed. *Abraham Lincoln's Speeches.* B.W. Dodge, 1895.

Current, Richard Nelson. *The Lincoln Nobody Knows.* McGraw-Hill, 1958.

Daugherty, James, ed. *Walt Whitman's America* (selections including "Portraits of Lincoln"). World, 1964.

De Regniers, Beatrice Schenck. *Abraham Lincoln Joke Book.* Random House, 1965.

Graebner, Norman Arthur. *Enduring Lincoln: Sesquicentennial Lectures at the University of Illinois.* Univ. of Illinois Press, 1959.

Gross, Anthony, ed. *Lincoln's Own Stories.* Harper & Brothers, 1912.

Harnsberger, Caroline Thomas. *The Lincoln Treasury.* Wilcox & Follett, 1950.

Herndon, William H. and Weik, Jesse W. *Lincoln: The True Story of a Great Life.* Pelford-Clarke, 1890.

———*Herndon's Life of Lincoln* (edited by Paul M. Angle). World, 1949.

Herndon, William. *The Hidden Lincoln* (edited by Emanual Hertz). Viking Press, 1938.

———*Herndon's Life of Lincoln.* DaCapo Press, 1983.

Hertz, Emanual. *Lincoln Talks: A Biography in Anecdote.* Viking Press, 1939.

Horgan, Paul. *Citizen of New Salem.* Farrar, Strauss and Cudahy, 1961.

House, Brant. *Lincoln's Wit.* Ace Books, 1958.

Jennison, Keith Warren. *Humorous Mr. Lincoln.* Crowell, 1965.

Kerner, Fred, ed. *Treasury of Lincoln Quotations.* Doubleday, 1965.

Lamon, Ward Hill. *The Life of Abraham Lincoln: From His Birth to His Inauguration as President.* A.C. McClurg, 1895.

Lang, Jack H. *Lincoln's Fireside Reading.* World, 1965.

Lapsley, Arthur Brooks, ed. *Writings of Abraham Lincoln.* Collier, 1905–06.

Lewis, Lloyd. *Myths after Lincoln.* Harcourt, Brace, 1929.

Masters, Edgar Lee. *Lincoln, the Man.* Dodd, Mead, 1931.

McClure, Alexander K. *Lincoln's Yarns and Stories.* John C. Winston, 1904.

Mearns, David Chambers. *Largely Lincoln.* St. Martin's Press, 1961.

Merwin, Roe, ed. *Speeches & Letters of Abraham Lincoln.* E.P. Dutton, 1894.

Morrow, Honore McCue Willsie. *The Lincoln Stories.* Morrow, 1934.

Nevins, Allan and Stone, Irving, eds. *Lincoln: A Contemporary Portrait.* Doubleday, 1962.

Newman, Ralph G. *Lincoln for the Ages.* Doubleday, 1960.

——*Abraham Lincoln: His Story in His Own Words.* Doubleday, 1970.

Nicolay, John G. and Hay, John, eds. *Complete Works of Abraham Lincoln* (12 vols.). Boy Rangers of America, 1894.

Oates, Stephen B. *Abraham Lincoln: The Man Behind the Myths.* Harper & Row, 1984.

——*With Malice Toward None: The Life of Abraham Lincoln.* Harper & Row, 1977.

Pattee, Fred Lewis. *Century Readings in American Literature.* Appleton, 1932.

——*First Century of American Literature.* Appleton, 1935.

Political Debates Between Hon. Abraham Lincoln and Hon. Stephen Douglas (entered according to Act of Congress, 1860). Follett, Foster, 1860.

Polley, Robert, ed. *Lincoln: His Words and His World* (compiled by editors of *Country Beautiful* magazine). Hawthorn Books, 1965.

Quarles, Benjamin. *Lincoln and the Negro.* Oxford Univ. Press, 1962.

Sandburg, Carl. *Abraham Lincoln: The Prairie Years* (2 vols.). Harcourt, Brace, 1926.

——*Abe Lincoln Grows Up.* Harcourt, Brace, 1928.

——*Abraham Lincoln: The War Years* (4 vols.). Harcourt, Brace, 1939.

Schauffler, Robert Haven, ed. *Lincoln's Birthday.* Moffat, Yard, 1909.

Scripps, John Locke. *Life of Abraham Lincoln.* Indiana Univ. Press, 1961.

Segal, Charles M. *Conversations with Lincoln.* Putnam, 1961.

Selby, Paul. *Anecdotal Lincoln*. Thomas & Thomas, 1900.

Shaw, Archer H., ed. *The Lincoln Encyclopedia*. Macmillan, 1950.

Stephenson, Nathaniel Wright, ed. *An Autobiography of Abraham Lincoln*. Bobbs-Merrill, 1926.

Van Doren, Carl, ed. *Literary Works of Abraham Lincoln*. Heritage Press, 1942.

Wolf, William. *The Almost Chosen People*. Doubleday, 1959.

Wordsworth, R.D., ed. *Abe Lincoln's Anecdotes and Stories*. Mutual, 1908.

Zali, Paul M. *Abe Lincoln Laughing*. Univ. of California Press, 1982.